LIVING LOVED

tiny wonder
PUBLISHING

LIVING LOVED

An 8-week journey to living fully loved

by Jamie Klusacek
with Hannah Grieser

Living Loved

Copyright © 2025 by Jamie Klusacek

All rights reserved. No part of this book may be used or reproduced in any manner whatsoever without written permission except in the case of brief quotations embodied in critical articles and reviews.

First published in the United States by Tiny Wonder Publishing
First Printing, 2025

ISBN: 978-1-7361181-8-4 Paperback
Library of Congress Control Number: 2024926686

Cover and Interior Design: Milan Klusacek

To all the girls, young and old, who need to remember just how loved they are by God. Let's learn to **Live Loved** together.

HOW TO USE THIS BOOK

This book is an 8-week journey to living fully loved.

Each week, we will focus on a Bible verse for you to meditate on and memorize as we explore the truth about what God says regarding our hearts. We'll dive into different translations and aspects of the verse to deepen our understanding. The weeks are made up of five daily readings based on scripture, daily prayers to help you develop the habit of listening and talking to God, and questions to inspire deeper introspection.

There are also spaces for you to take notes. Have fun with it! Grab some new highlighters, write in the margins, and jot down what God is speaking to you personally about why your heart matters and how to live fully loved according to His Word. Underline the things that stand out to you. Embrace the journey.

Sprinkled throughout, you'll also find inspirational quotes from men and women who love Jesus and love YOU. Remember, you aren't alone on this journey. You are surrounded by people who are cheering for God's best in your life. Enjoy!

Foreword

In 2016, THERE{4} Gathering was born with a singular purpose: to have a lasting impact on the next generation of teen girls. Since then, we have witnessed the incredible transformation of thousands of girls at our live conferences and countless more around the world through livestream views. Our ministry has flourished with the combination of exceptional teachers, dynamic worship, and a community of amazing girls. However, at the core of everything we do lies the unshakable foundation of God's Word.

The devotional you're holding in your hands is more than just a book. It is a roadmap designed to guide you on your journey of walking with and towards Jesus in every aspect of your life. While it does not seek to replace the Bible, it serves as a friendly mentor to lead you deeper into the heart of Jesus through His Word.

Within these pages, you will find daily reflections and thought-provoking insights that encourage spiritual growth. Each entry beckons you to spend intentional time with God, allowing His truth to permeate your heart and mind. As you devote yourself to these readings, may the words inspire and challenge you to embrace a life lived for Jesus.

We are honored to walk alongside you in this journey of faith. Our hope is that you will use this devotional, not merely as a guide, but as a constant reminder of the transforming power of God's Word. May it encourage you, strengthen you, and equip you to impact the world around you. Let's embark on this adventure together, as we let God's truth shape our lives, illuminate our path, and compel us to live out His purposes each day.

With love and anticipation for the great things God will do through you,

Tiffany Daniels
Founder and Visionary, THERE{4} Gathering

♡ Preface

You are fully loved—and you weren't meant to journey alone.

Before you begin reading this devotional, I want you to know that in order to live a life that's fully loved—in order to receive God's love, love Him well in return, and experience the overflow of His promises from living in God's type of love—we need help from the Holy Spirit.

In John 14:26, Jesus says that He is going to give us a helper in the form of the Holy Spirit. As soon as you accept Jesus as your Lord and Savior, you have full access to the Holy Spirit. Here's what the Holy Spirit does for you and me:

The Holy Spirit is available to all believers, empowering them and bringing light to the dark places in their lives. The Holy Spirit remains with them, freely giving them spiritual knowledge, aid, and comfort while setting them apart for God's special purpose. The Holy Spirit also prays with us and for us, intervening on our behalf.

We have the Holy Spirit to guide us, teach us, and give us the power we need to accomplish what seems impossible. He wants to help us Live Loved.

Let's start out by asking Him to be a part of our journey.

Holy Spirit, please help guide me on this journey of living fully loved in You. Sometimes I have a hard time receiving love and giving love. Throughout this study, would You give me the power to embrace what it means to live loved according to Your Word and to experience the fruit that comes with it? Thank You for Your help.

Jamie Kay Klusacek
Author

CONTENTS

8   How to use this book

11   Letter from the Founder

13   Preface

16   {Week 1} Let's talk about your heart

34   {Week 2} Let's talk about who you love first

52   {Week 3} Let's talk about God's Word in your heart

70   {Week 4} Let's talk about who you trust first

88	{Week 5} Let's talk about when your heart hurts
106	{Week 6} Let's talk about being filled with peace
124	{Week 7} Let's talk about your deepest desires
142	{Week 8} Let's talk about what comes out of your heart
163	Salvation Prayer
164	About the Authors
169	Acknowledgments
171	Photography
172	Footnotes
174	Other Resources

let's talk about

YOUR HEART

verse to memorize

"Guard your heart above all else, for it determines the course of your life."

—Proverbs 4:23, NLT

DAY 1

"GUARD YOUR **HEART** ABOVE ALL ELSE, FOR IT DETERMINES THE COURSE OF YOUR LIFE."

—PROVERBS 4:23, NLT

Your heart is precious, and the only person who deserves the right to hold it is someone who knows its value. Someone who will care for it. Protect it. Love and nurture it. Someone who regards it as cherished. Someone who recognizes the beautiful creation you are and the amazing purpose destined for your life. That's the only person who should have the right to hold your heart.

Giving ownership of our hearts to the RIGHT PERSON is how we start to live fully loved.

And the thing is, we decide who we will give our hearts to. If we want to live loved—not for a semester or a season, but throughout our lifetime—we must give our hearts to the only One who sees who we truly are and loves us fiercely in spite of ourselves. His name is Jesus. He is our only worthy option.

To start off this week, we need to ask ourselves a question—and we need to be brutally honest in how we answer. Otherwise, we won't have a solid foundation to build on. So here is the question: Who holds your heart?

Before you answer, let me clarify what "heart" actually means in Proverbs 4:23. Some of us may think that heart is just another term for gushy feelings, goosebumps, or inner desires, but it's so much more than that.

The word **heart** in Hebrew is usually referring to some aspect of the inner self. It's considered to be the seat of our inner nature, as well as everything else on the inside—our mind, will, emotions, feelings, and intellect.

That's worth repeating. Our heart is almost everything within us. Thoughts.

Feelings. Emotions. Intellect. Living within our hearts are the things that matter to us. And the Bible tells us that from our heart, the course of our life is determined. That sounds like a pretty important thing.

Our heart is our most cherished possession. So let's make sure the one who holds it is worthy and capable of such an honor.

PRAYER

God, I want You to hold my heart. Help me see how important my heart is and that giving it to You is the best decision I could ever make.

BRING IT HOME

What are some things I've given my heart to other than God?

let's talk about your heart

DAY 2

"GOD IS **LOVE**."
—1 JOHN 4:8, NKJV

If we are going to give our hearts to someone—to live life in a fully loved way—I think we should understand what kind of love this world has to offer and what kind of love God has to offer. Because living loved is more than a feeling; it's rooted in a type of love only God can give.

It is believed that Jesus understood three languages: Hebrew, Aramaic, and Greek.[1] The New Testament was written in Koine Greek, which is actually a dead language today (meaning no one still speaks it).[2] Although the English language basically uses one word to describe various types of love, Koine Greek has four different words for love.

First, there's **eros** love. This is a passionate, sensual, physical type of love. It is romantic love. Then there is **philia** love. This is a friendship love, often used to describe the type of bond that goes deeper than a casual friend. The third type of love is **storge** love. This is the love, affection, or bond between family.

These three types of love can fade with time and seem to be dependent on the placement you hold in another person's life. They can leave us asking questions like: What if I do something wrong and I'm not loved anymore? And that can be scary.

The love that God uses to describe who He is and the love He has for you is different from any of these. It's **agape** love. In Greek, **agape** love is the highest, purest form of love. It shows selfless, sacrificial, unconditional care for others. It goes beyond feelings and is shown in action and commitment. It's love as a choice, not out of obligation, attraction, or feelings.

This is the kind of love God has for you. It's not casual or flippant. It doesn't fade with time. It's love as a choice. A love that is selfless, sacrificial, compassionate, and full of care. A love that will **always choose you**. It's agape love.

When God pursues you with His love and you give your heart to Him, this is the type of love He will love you with. Giving your heart to the One with the purest love for you is the only pathway to living fully loved. God is that kind of love.

PRAYER

God, thank You for loving me with agape love. A love that is not dependent on what I do, but who You are. Thank You for being love.

BRING IT HOME

How does understanding agape love affect my relationship with God?

God, thank You for loving me with *agape* love.

selfless & unconditional

purest form of love

doesn't fade with time

not based on feelings

DAY 3

"KEEP YOUR HEART WITH ALL DILIGENCE, FOR OUT OF IT **SPRINGS THE ISSUES OF LIFE.**"

—PROVERBS 4:23, NKJV

Let's dig a little deeper into why your heart is so important. Have you ever wondered what your life will be like in five or ten years? I'm sure you have hopes and dreams; we all do. But maybe you also have fears and worries of what could be. I know I do. I mean, we all hope that our lives will turn out good, but can we actually have assurance that they will?

The Bible says that out of the heart springs or flows the issues of life. The heart affects all that you are. What you say. What you do. How you view yourself. Even where your life is headed. It's like your heart is a pathway to living the life you've always dreamed. A pathway to living loved.

The term "issues of life" or "**wellspring** of life" is so interesting. In Hebrew, it can be translated: exit, boundary, source, border, direction, end, escape, farthest extent.

The Bible is telling us that the heart is what sets the boundaries in our lives. It is the source of our life. It's the thing that determines the farthest extent of where we will go and what we will do. It determines the direction of our lives.

I don't know about you, but oftentimes I can't be trusted with determining the right path for my life. That's a lot of pressure to hold. The great news is, we don't need to hold that pressure. We weren't meant to have everything figured out. By giving our hearts fully to Jesus, we are giving Him the right to choose what's best for us.

We control who has access to our hearts—and when it's Jesus, we can trust that He will direct our lives on a pathway that is perfect for us.

PRAYER

God, I give You my heart again today. As I give it to You, I know You promise to help guide and direct my life towards Your best. Thank You.

BRING IT HOME

If my heart is the source of my life, what is flowing out of it?

DAY 4

> "THE THIEF DOES NOT COME EXCEPT TO STEAL, AND TO KILL, AND TO DESTROY. I HAVE COME THAT **THEY MAY HAVE LIFE**, AND THAT THEY MAY HAVE IT MORE ABUNDANTLY."
>
> —JOHN 10:10, NKJV

Are you starting to realize the importance of your heart? I want you to understand that you can trust God with your heart and His purpose for your life. And truly, I don't just want you to understand it—I want you to be fully persuaded that placing your heart in the hands of Jesus is the BEST way you could ever live.

In order to do that, we are going back to scripture so you can understand who Jesus is and what His heart is for your life. When you place your heart in His hands, what kind of life does He have in mind for you? Will it even be something you like? Let's find out together.

In John 10:10, Jesus says that He has come to give you life, more abundant life, but what does that actually mean? We are already living and breathing, so what kind of life can Jesus give that we don't already have? Get ready to have your mind blown.

The word **life** in Greek means physical and human life, as well as the eternal life of bliss and glory in the kingdom of God for Christians. BUT it also means living a blessed life, a life that satisfies.

So get this: Jesus hasn't just come to give us living, breathing life; He's also come to give us a promise of eternal life with Him. And to top it all off, He wants to give us a life on earth that's blessed and truly satisfying. He wants us to live a life that is absolutely, 100% fulfilling on the inside.

But He doesn't stop there. He wants to give us abundant life. The word used for **abundantly** in Greek means: superabundant in quantity and superior in quality. It's a sense of beyond, having an advantage beyond measure. WOW.

This is the kind of life that God has destined for you and me. We can trust Him with our hearts. And when we do, we begin to experience the fully loved life He has in store for us.

PRAYER

God, I want the kind of life that only You can give. It's an abundant life flowing from the inside out. Would You help me to live in Your type of life?

BRING IT HOME

How does understanding the kind of life God has for me help me trust God more?

God's love for me is based on:

~~My performance~~

~~How lovable I feel~~

~~If I'm doing enough to earn it~~

~~How often I go to church~~

God's grace

"This is real love—not that we loved God, but that he loved us and sent his Son as a sacrifice to take away our sins." –1 John 4:10, NLT

# DAY 5

"THE THIEF'S PURPOSE IS TO **STEAL** AND KILL AND **DESTROY**. MY PURPOSE IS TO GIVE THEM A RICH AND SATISFYING LIFE."
—JOHN 10:10, NLT

God's intent for you is to give you a rich and satisfying life. That's what happens when He holds your heart. You begin to live that life you didn't even know you needed—a life lived fully loved. If you give your heart to anything or anyone else, other than God first, it will not lead to the fully loved life you want to live.

Let me say, God holding your heart does not mean everything will always go your way. It doesn't mean that you won't have hardships or difficulties, because you will— that's just life. But it does mean that your heart—who you are on the inside—can and will continue to flourish, because Jesus holds your heart.

So we know what God's purpose is for your life. Now let's look at what the devil tries to do instead. The Bible tells us not to be ignorant of the devil's devices in 2 Corinthians 2:11, so we are going to take a closer look at what the devil wants to do in your life. Specifically, I want to look at two words from John 10:10: steal and destroy.

The word **steal** in Greek is translated as "filch." If you're like me, you have no idea what "filch" means in English. I had to look it up, and it means this: to steal secretly or casually. Meaning, the devil wants to take something that belongs to you without your permission, especially secretly, by force or gradually over time.

The word **destroy** in Greek means to cause to perish, or put to death, BUT it also means "to bring to naught, render void the wisdom of the wise; ... to destroy in the middle..."

Oh my goodness. The devil wants to destroy the fully loved life God has in store for you. He wants to destroy the work that God has begun in you before it's done. The devil's desire is to secretly take what is rightfully yours in Christ— the full, abundant, purpose-filled, fully loved life that God has intended for you. Love, joy, peace, patience, kindness, goodness, faithfulness, and self-control are fruits of the Spirit God wants flowing from the inside of you as you give your heart to Him.

The devil can't be trusted with our hearts, but God can. Don't let him rob from you what is rightfully yours in Christ.

PRAYER

God, would You give me an awareness of when the devil is trying to steal from me? I want to choose You and live a life following You with all my heart.

BRING IT HOME

Am I allowing the devil to steal things that are rightfully mine in Christ? If so, what is he stealing?

Let's talk about

WHO YOU LOVE FIRST

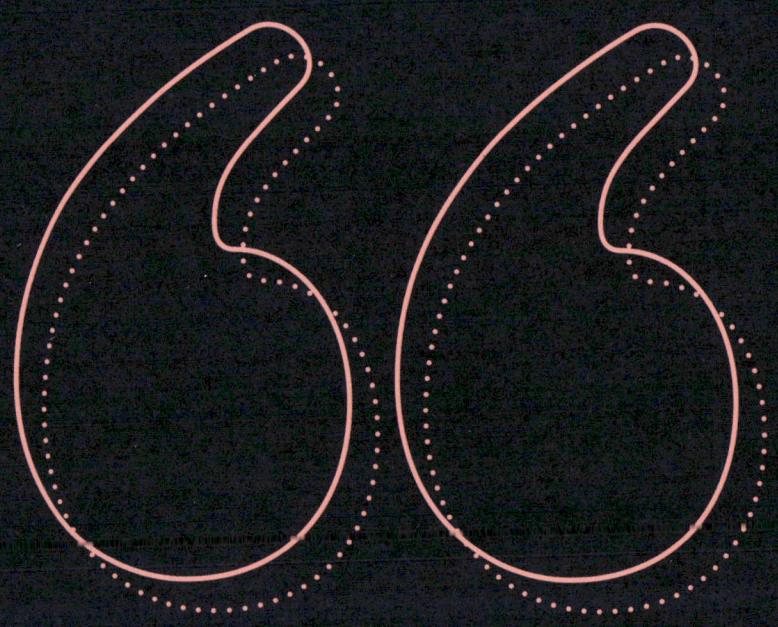

Jesus replied, 'You must love the Lord your God with all your heart, all your soul, and all your mind.' This is the first and greatest commandment. A second is equally important: 'Love your neighbor as yourself.'"

—Matthew 22:37-39, NLT

meditate on this week

DAY 1

"JESUS REPLIED, 'YOU MUST LOVE THE LORD YOUR GOD WITH ALL YOUR **HEART**...'"

—MATTHEW 22:37-39, NLT

This word for "heart" in this verse is a little deeper than the word we talked about last week in Proverbs 4. The word here for **heart** in Greek can mean so many things. It's the place where desires, feelings, and impulses in the heart and mind are born. Phrases like "from the heart" mean that you willingly do something with your whole heart and soul. It's the center of your values, affections, passions, intellect and understanding.

The heart is the intangible you, expressed by what you do. It's what you think about. What you meditate on. It's your beliefs about yourself, God, and others. It's the framework from which you view and experience the world. And what does God ask us to do with our hearts? He asks us to love Him first.

You see, in this passage, Jesus is being tested by the Pharisees. The Pharisees were a group of religious people who valued the law of Moses. This law started out with ten commandments from God, but in Jewish tradition they taught that there are 613 commandments that were binding for the Jewish people to obey.[3] That's a lot of rules to remember!

Jesus takes all of these commandments and filters them into two basic principles: love God and love others. He tells them that everything else in life hangs on these two principles. He refocuses their attention away from a list of do's and don'ts and onto their relationships. **It's all about relationships.**

Maybe you're just starting your journey with God and you think that Christianity is about keeping a set of rules so that you can be in right standing with God. I have great news for you: You can be in right standing with God because Jesus paid the price for your sins. The moment you accept Him into your life, you are standing in His righteousness, not your own.

Instead of focusing on a list of rules, start focusing on loving God with all your heart. Everything else will flow out of that relationship. We love Him because He first loved us.[4] Loving Jesus is how we start to live fully loved. It's all about the relationship.

PRAYER

God, I admit that sometimes I focus on the rules of following You more than loving You. Help me focus on our relationship first and know that You will help me with the rest.

BRING IT HOME

How can I focus on loving God this week?

wk.2 DAY 2

"JESUS REPLIED, 'YOU MUST LOVE THE LORD YOUR GOD...'"
—MATTHEW 22:37, NLT

Love can be a tricky word to think about. I mean, when you think about the word love what's the first thing that comes to your mind? Maybe it's the way your dad loves your mom. Or maybe it's more of the feeling you get towards that guy—the butterflies and goosebumps. Maybe that's true love. So when God says to love Him with all your heart, does that mean you don't love Him if you don't have those feelings?

Remember how we talked about the word "agape" in week one? We learned that God is love, but He's not just any kind of love. He's agape love. Here's a refresher on what that word means.

Agape love is the highest, most pure form of love. It embodies selflessness, sacrifice and unconditional care for others. It goes beyond feelings and is shown in action and commitment. It's love as a choice, not out of obligation, attraction, or feelings.

The word for love used in this passage is the same type of love that describes who God is. God isn't asking us to love Him based on our feelings or because we had goosebumps in His presence at an amazing conference. He's asking us to **agape love** Him as a choice. To choose to love Him when we feel like it and when we don't. It's a decision to love, trust, and give our hearts to Him even when everything in us doesn't want to.

This kind of love may seem wonderful to receive, but over-the-top hard to give. I'm so thankful to God that we don't need to cultivate this type of agape love on our own! God sent a helper to teach us how to love Him fully—it's the Holy Spirit. When we make the decision to follow Jesus, we have the Holy Spirit as our helper and guide.

If you want to learn to love God with this agape love, just ask. He is always willing to help.

PRAYER

God, I need Your help learning to love You. I know that the more I experience and understand Your love for me, the easier it is to love You in return. Help me to receive Your love for me.

BRING IT HOME

How can I show God how much I love Him?

"Spread love everywhere you go. Let no one ever come to you without leaving happier."

—Mother Teresa

DAY 3

"AND YOU MUST LOVE THE LORD YOUR GOD WITH ALL YOUR **HEART**, ALL YOUR **SOUL**, ALL YOUR **MIND**, AND ALL YOUR **STRENGTH**."

—MARK 12:30, NLT

I love the gospel of Mark's version of this same story because he adds another word to the list of how we should love God. We are learning what it means to love God with all our heart, but let's take a look at what it means to love God with all our soul, mind, and strength.

The word **soul** in Greek means your entire affection. Affection is usually shown to something or someone that you are attached or devoted to. When God says to love Him with all your soul He wants you to be devoted to Him first in your life.

The word **mind** in Greek means your deep thoughts. It also means what you meditate on, your imagination, and your understanding. So, Jesus is asking us to love Him even in our deep thoughts, imagination, and understanding. Sometimes we don't always understand God's plan, but we can trust Him beyond our understanding because we know He's a good God.

I want to bring my imaginations and dreams to Him first. In fact, I want my imaginations to line up with what He says about me in His Word. If I'm going to daydream about anything, I want God to be part of that process. I invite Him into my mind because He cares about every detail of my life, even what I think about. And His thoughts towards me are greater than mine.[5]

The word **strength** in Greek means your ability or might. It's the power and strength of both your body and mind. God doesn't just want us to love Him with our hearts and the things on the inside—He also wants us to love Him with our strength and our actions. Someone could tell you they love you a thousand times, but showing you makes all the difference in the world. As the old saying goes, "Actions speak louder than words."

God wants every part of you, because He loves every part of you. When we accept His love and get His help to love Him in return, it places us on a pathway to living the fully loved life we were meant to live.

PRAYER

God, I know You love every part of me. Help me to give You every part of me, not just the parts I'm proud of. I want to live a fully loved life in You.

BRING IT HOME

How can I love God with all my heart, soul, mind, and strength?

Let's talk about who you love first

DAY 4

> "SO NOW I AM GIVING YOU A NEW COMMANDMENT: **LOVE EACH OTHER**. JUST AS I HAVE LOVED YOU, YOU SHOULD LOVE EACH OTHER. YOUR LOVE FOR ONE ANOTHER WILL PROVE TO THE WORLD THAT YOU ARE MY DISCIPLES."
>
> —JOHN 13:34-35, NLT

In the verse we are meditating on this week, Jesus says that the second greatest commandment is to love your neighbor. You can't fully love God, receive His love, and give your heart to Him without it affecting the way you treat others. It's impossible. The more we understand the love God has for us, the more love for others oozes out of every facet of our being.

Chapters 13-18 in the gospel of John are considered the last discourse of Jesus—meaning, this is the last full-on conversation Jesus had with His best friends before He went to die on the cross for our sins. What He says in these chapters holds weight and significance—and the words still matter to us today.

The first thing we see in these final moments of Jesus' life here on earth is Him serving others. He begins the last dinner with His closest friends by washing their feet. Before you're tempted to think that's not a big deal, know that in Jesus' time, washing someone's feet was a job for a slave. It was undignified. When you came to someone's home with filthy, sweaty feet, a servant was meant to wash them, not the guest of honor. Jesus took the role of a servant.[6]

After this shocking act of humility and love, Jesus drops this one-liner that has echoed throughout history: **"Your love for one another will prove to the world that you are my disciples."**

When you live fully loved, some things start to naturally overflow from your life—you just can't help it. One of those things is love.

We cannot truly receive God's love and live fully loved without love flowing out of us onto others. The two things are always linked together—they're impossible to separate. In fact, there is one way people will know we are Christians, and it's not because we say we are. It's not because we carry our Bible with us everywhere we go, write "God loves you" on our Starbucks receipt, or listen to our Bible App—although those are all great things.

People will know we are Christians because of our love for one another. Loving God shows itself by loving others—not just loving the people we enjoy, but also respecting and loving those we don't like very much.

It's a truth we can't escape. Love is the overflow of living loved.

PRAYER

God, I really want to experience and receive Your love for me. As I do, help me learn how to love others. I need Your help, Holy Spirit.

BRING IT HOME

When I look at my life honestly, do I show God's love to others? Why or why not?

DAY 5

"A SECOND IS EQUALLY IMPORTANT: 'LOVE YOUR NEIGHBOR AS **YOURSELF**.'"

—MATTHEW 22:39, NLT

Learn to love yourself. It's hard to let God's love flow out of you when you are constantly comparing yourself with others, never content with who God created you to be.

Loving yourself does not mean that you are selfish, vain, stuck-up, mean, and prideful, always putting your needs and wants above others. What it does mean is that you love and accept the unique creation God has made you to be. It also means, practically, that you should love others in the same way that you care for yourself and want what's best for your life.

Let's talk about loving your uniqueness. Sometimes loving yourself can be difficult. It's easy to look around and become discontent with who God created YOU to be. You might wish you looked like the girl next door, had as many friends as the people you follow on Instagram, lived in the model home down the street, had the charming personality of the popular girls at school, or were an all-star athlete instead of feeling like you have two left feet.

Jesus is clear: He created you on purpose, with purpose—just the way you are! Psalm 139:13 says that He "made all the delicate, inner parts of my body and knit me together in my mother's womb." He took care to fashion you, every part of you—your looks, temperament, disposition, passions, and personality—because He loves you so much.

When we live constantly discontent with who He made us to be, it's like we are at war with ourselves—and honestly, that feels hard. It's like trying to use your cell phone as a spoon. Yeah, it might work awkwardly for a bit—but eventually, eating off your cell phone would have some serious drawbacks, and you'd end up damaging the phone and hindering its intended use.

Some of us are made to be cell phones, but we want to be spoons. We have lived our entire lives trying to be something we aren't. Fully loved daughter, it's time to start loving the person God created YOU to be.

As we discover who we are through God's Word and embrace the unique creation He has called us to be, God can help us see that the best person we could ever be is ourselves.

PRAYER

God, sometimes it's hard to love myself. While You are perfect, when I look at myself, I just see how I don't measure up to others. Help me see myself the way You see me and embrace who You created me to be.

BRING IT HOME

What's one thing unique about myself that I love?

Let's talk about who you love first

live

"Living original means being confident that God made you in a really cool, unique way."

—Sadie Robertson

original

let's talk about

GOD'S WORD IN YOUR HEART

memorize this week

"I have <u>hidden</u> your word in my (heart,) that I might not sin against you."

—Psalm 119:11, NLT

DAY 1

"I HAVE **HIDDEN** YOUR WORD IN MY HEART, THAT I MIGHT NOT SIN AGAINST YOU."
—PSALM 119:11, NLT

Knowing who God is, what His plan is for our lives, and who we are in Him helps us live in the fully loved zone. But it's hard to love first and give our hearts to a God we don't know. So how can we get to know God when we can't see, touch, or hear Him? I've got an answer to that question and it's super simple: We get to know Him through the Bible.

The Bible is like an autobiography and biography all wrapped into one. It's the most unique book written in all of history. It tells us all about who God is through the lives of His people and through divine inspiration from the Holy Spirit. We may not be able to literally see God, but as we get to know Him through scripture—and understand how He moved in the lives of those in the Bible—we see a blueprint for how to recognize God in our own lives and in the world around us.

If we want to live in the fully-loved-by-God space, we have to develop a relationship with Him. As you study scriptures, you will start to see that God doesn't just want you to have book knowledge of Him. God wants to walk with you throughout your day. He wants to help you with those tough decisions. He wants to be there to comfort you when you've had the worst day ever. He cares about your hopes, dreams, and epic failures. It's a journey with Him, not a crash-course test you take once and either pass or fail. He wants to be your best friend.

The Psalmist, King David, says that he hides God's Word in his heart. This word **hidden** means to hide by covering over, to hoard or reserve, to protect or lay up; secret place, to store up hidden treasure. David is saying that he takes God's Word and hides it in the secret, precious places of his heart. Why? So that he won't sin against God.

Sin can be a scary word, but it shouldn't be. It simply means to miss the mark, fail, or do something wrong according to God's standards. That's it, plain and simple. And you know what? We all sin! David is saying that treasuring God's Word will help him choose God's best in the decisions he faces in life.

The more you know God through His Word, the more you'll realize His ways will lead you to the fully loved life you want to live.

PRAYER

God, sometimes when I read Your Word, it goes in one ear and out the other. I want to learn who You are. Help me to not just read Your Word, but learn to treasure it in my heart.

BRING IT HOME

What is one practical way I can create a habit of treasuring God's Word?

Let's talk about God's Word in your heart

DAY 2

*"SINCE WE ARE HIS **CHILDREN**, WE ARE HIS HEIRS. IN FACT, TOGETHER WITH CHRIST WE ARE HEIRS OF GOD'S GLORY."*

—ROMANS 8:17, NLT

As we read the Bible and learn to treasure God's ways, it will help direct our paths on what's best for our lives—God's plan. And in the process, we will get to know the God who loves us beyond anything we could ever imagine. But you know what else you will find as you read God's Word? You'll find out who YOU are.

As we hide God's Word in our hearts, we find out about ourselves too. God has a lot to say about who you are. Now, there are hundreds of things He says about you in His Word. Hundreds of promises He has for your life. But the thing I love most about everything He says about our identity is that we are His children.

This word **children** in Greek means child, daughter, or son, but it also has a deeper meaning. It's talking about someone who is the object of a parent's love and care. It's the tender term God has for you. Now, you may not have had the best parents in the world. Maybe you've even been hurt by your parents. But God is not like your earthly family. He is your heavenly Father—which means that He is the perfect picture of what a parent should, but never could, fully be.

Imagine a Dad who knows every detail of your life, who created you with a specific purpose in mind. He took time to create the exact color of your eyes and hair—and for some of you, those tiny freckles that grace your nose. This Dad is over-the-moon for you just the way you are. He knows your temperament, likes, dislikes, and everything in between. He has been there for your victorious moments of triumph and your secret places of defeat—and loves you greater still. He's a Dad who loves to hear your voice, even when it seems like nonsense. A Dad who values your input, ideas, and creativity—because that's the unique way He made you. No problem is too big or too small, He wants a place in it all.

Why? Because this is a Dad who cares for you—deeply, truly, fully, heart all-in. And He knows your life was made to experience the type of love and care that only He could give. This is the kind of heavenly Dad you have in God.

Before you are anything else, you are God's child. Remember that. Let it sink in. It is such a gift. It's not dependent on what you do; it's about who you are, and that will never change. With that comes a promise that He will take full responsibility to love and care for your life no matter what.

Hiding God's Word in your heart means that you find out who you are. You are a child of God.

PRAYER

God, help me to understand who You are and who I am through the light of Your Word. Direct me to passages I need to hear so that my heart is shaped by You.

BRING IT HOME

What's one thing I'm learning from God's Word about myself?

"I'm not valuable for what I do. I'm valuable for who He made me to be."

–Katie Davis Majors

DAY 3

*"FOR THE WORD OF GOD IS LIVING AND POWERFUL, **SHARPER THAN ANY TWO-EDGED SWORD**, PIERCING EVEN TO THE DIVISION OF SOUL AND SPIRIT, AND OF JOINT AND MARROW, AND IS A DISCERNER OF THE THOUGHTS AND INTENTS OF THE HEART."*

—HEBREWS 4:12, NKJV

At this point, you might be saying: "Oh my goodness, I really want to get to know God and who He's created me to be, but I barely know the Bible. I feel like I'm falling short. Even though I'm reading the Bible a little, how do I know that God's Word is actually in my heart?"

I've got good news for you—I don't have the entire Bible memorized either! Start small. Read God's Word daily. Memorize a verse a week, or even one a month. God's Word will start to affect your heart and the Holy Spirit will help guide you.

We talked earlier about what our heart really is. I want to make a connection between your heart and your mind because they walk hand-in-hand in your life. As we've learned, the word "heart" in scripture usually refers to the things inside us: the center of our mind, desires, affections, will, feelings, intellect, and emotion. Your heart is also what's in your mind.

In the passage above, the Bible tells us that the Word of God is a weapon for your heart and mind. In Jesus' day, a **two-edged sword** was a special type of weapon. It was a sword that could cut and pierce every contact point quickly, deeply, and more accurately than any other type of sword.[7]

So how do you know if what's in your heart and mind are from God? Use the Bible. As you hide God's Word in your heart, the Bible will be a tool to help you discern what God's best is for you and learn to cut the rest off.

God's Word can and will help guide you towards living a life that's fully loved in Christ.

PRAYER

God, I know that my heart and mind are connected and that Your Word will help me discern what decisions are of You and what aren't. Help me to learn Your ways through Your Word.

BRING IT HOME

What does God's Word as a two-edged sword mean to me? Are there things I'm thinking about that don't line up with God's Word? If so, what are they?

DAY 4

"BUT THE WISDOM THAT IS FROM ABOVE IS FIRST **PURE**, THEN **PEACEABLE**, **GENTLE**, WILLING TO YIELD, FULL OF MERCY AND GOOD FRUITS, WITHOUT PARTIALITY AND WITHOUT HYPOCRISY."

—JAMES 3:17, NKJV

Today, we are going to talk about the connection between our heart and mind. We will learn to discern if what we are thinking about ourselves and others is wisdom from God or just the product of a midnight Ben and Jerry's ice cream binge.

In those moments when you're thinking about your decisions, stewing in thoughts about yourself, contemplating telling your friend off for the way they hurt you, or wondering if you should speak up about what's churning inside you—first ask yourself if it's pure, peaceable, and gentle.

Pure just means modest, perfect, and clear. Sometimes I'm thinking thoughts that aren't very pure about someone else and I'm tempted to give them a backhanded compliment that is really a tear-down because I'm offended by them. So before I speak, I try to ask myself: Is this coming from a pure motive on the inside of me? Do I have their best interest at heart, and does it align with the clarity I find in scripture?

Next let's ask ourselves if our thoughts are **peaceable** and **gentle**. To be peaceable is the opposite of war and dissension. It's harmony and peace of mind. It also means peace on the inside that comes "from reconciliation with God and a sense of divine favor." It's knowing that you're worthy of happiness. I don't know about you, but it's crazy easy for me to think negative thoughts about myself. Thoughts about how much better I could/should/must do or be. Thoughts that there is no way I'm worthy of happiness. Have you ever been there?

When I put the thoughts of my mind and intentions of my heart under the light of James 3:17-18, it brings a lot of clarity. I ask myself: Is this thought in my heart bringing peace and harmony to myself and others? Is it coming out of a sense of God's favor and how worthy I am in His sight? If not, according to this verse—I kick that thought to the curb!

When examining your thoughts, first think: Is this pure, peaceable, and gentle? Is this how I would like to be treated? Is this how I should be treating others? If it's not, then don't let it set up permanent residence in your mind.

When our hearts and mind are in alignment with God, it helps us step into the fully loved life He has planned for us.

PRAYER
God, help me to have a heart and mind that is pure, peaceable, and gentle.

BRING IT HOME
How does knowing God's heart for my thought life help direct me towards making the right choices?

# DAY 5

"BUT THE WISDOM FROM ABOVE IS FIRST PURE, THEN PEACEABLE, GENTLE, **WILLING TO YIELD**, FULL OF **MERCY** AND GOOD FRUITS, **WITHOUT PARTIALITY** AND **WITHOUT HYPOCRISY**."

—JAMES 3:17, NKJV

The next piece of this verse that we are going to focus on is that wisdom from God is willing to **yield**. Now this word may not mean what you think it means. Being willing to yield doesn't mean that you're a pushover to every person that comes into your life. That would be exhausting. Instead, it means you know when to say, "I've been thinking about that thing all wrong—God, You're right!" It's about asking yourself if you're willing to exchange God's thoughts for your faulty ones. Can you receive sound wisdom from others? Sometimes we think our ways are the best ways. Being willing to yield means that we admit we don't know what's best for our lives at all times—we need God's help.

Next, James tells us that wisdom from God is full of mercy and good fruits. **Mercy** is active pity. It means that you are showing compassion to others. In fact, mercy says that even though you have a right to punish someone because what they did was wrong, you're choosing to pass over that deserved punishment. It's showing compassion to your sister even though she's worn your favorite shirt a million times without asking. It's giving others what they don't deserve.

The last two roadmaps to wisdom from God are: without partiality or hypocrisy. God's wisdom is **without partiality**—meaning that we aren't actively looking for faults in others—and **without hypocrisy**, meaning that we aren't pretending to be something we are not.

Hypocrisy is living with a mask on. It's pretending to be something we are not based on what we think other people want from us. We simply play a role instead of being who we really are, perhaps because it feels safer that way. We tell half-truths by revealing or concealing part of the truth just to make ourselves look better. We may feel like we are protecting ourselves by living with a mask on—but in reality, it's draining and will do more harm than good. It was never the way God intended you to live.

Hide this verse in your heart and come back to it. When you're wondering if what your heart is meditating on is from God, ask yourself: Is it pure, peaceable, gentle, willing to yield, full of mercy and good fruits, and without hypocrisy? All of these are markers that your thoughts and decisions are on the right track, leading you toward living your best life in God and living fully loved.

PRAYER

God, sometimes I'm tempted to hide parts of who I am and act like I'm something I'm not. When that happens, would You help me remain true to who You have created me to be?

BRING IT HOME

In what ways do I hide parts of who I am from others? Why?

Dear God,
When I'm tempted to hide parts of who I am and act like I'm something I'm not, would You help me remain true to who You have created me to be?

—me

Let's talk about

WHO YOU TRUST FIRST

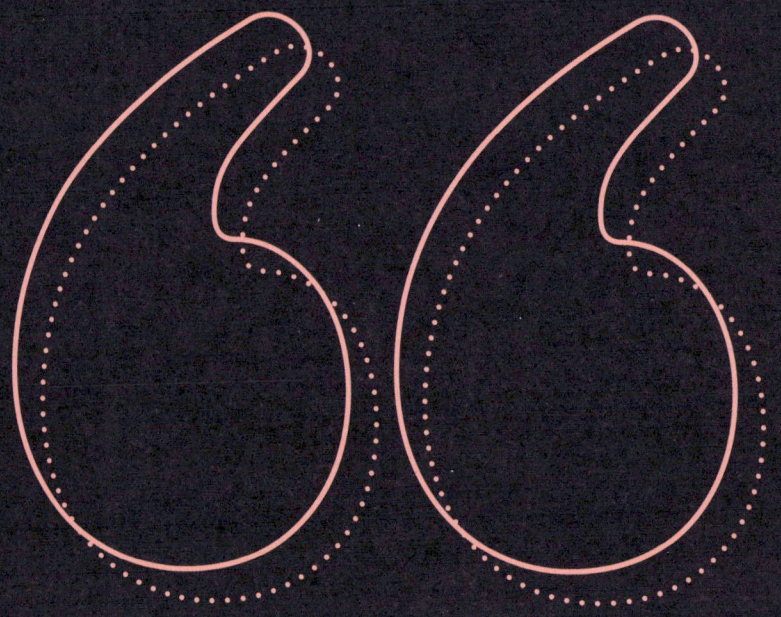

Trust in the Lord with all your (heart,) and lean not on your own understanding; In all your ways acknowledge Him, and He shall direct your path."

–Proverbs 3:5-6, NKJV

meditate on this week

DAY 1

"TRUST IN THE LORD
WITH ALL YOUR HEART..."
—PROVERBS 3:5, NLT

You can't have true love without trust. In any loving relationship, you need to have confidence in the other person's words and actions, and they need to be able to do the same with you. Still, people will let us down, and we will let other people down. Thankfully we can always trust the Lord to take care of us!

That's why Proverbs 3:5 says "Trust in the Lord with all your heart." It's a safe bet! The more we trust in God, the deeper our love with Him can grow. A big part of living loved is trusting that God sees you, guides you, and has great plans for your life. The Hebrew word for **trust** relates to the state of being confident, secure, and without fear. It means "to lie helpless, facedown." It's the feeling of safety that comes when you can fully rely on someone else.

Imagine going for a swim in the ocean and being unable to see the bottom. You can either spend your time worrying about what's beneath the surface and trying not to step on any creepy crawlies—or you can float on your back, letting the sun bask on your face, feeling at peace, and trusting that you are safe in the palm of God's hand.

Our relationship with God is a lot like that. He meets us in amazing ways as we allow ourselves to trust Him. Even when we don't understand what He's doing through our circumstances and are tempted to fear the unknown, we can choose to trust Him knowing He has our best interest at heart in relation to His Kingdom.

Matthew 8:23-27 tells a story of how we can trust Jesus even when everything feels chaotic. Jesus and His disciples were on a boat together when an intense storm suddenly hit them. This wasn't just any storm–it was a tempest, which had the fury of a tornado. While this was going on, Jesus was asleep! So, the disciples woke Him up and said, "Lord, save us! We're going to drown!" Jesus wasn't rattled. Matthew 8:26 says, "Then he got up and rebuked the wind and waves, and suddenly there was a great calm."

We can listen to the storm, or we can trust in God and experience "a great calm." What will you choose?

PRAYER

God, thank You for being so trustworthy! Today, I trust that You will keep me safe because You care for me. Help me recognize when I'm paying more attention to the chaos than I am to Your voice. I choose to lean into Your love and embrace the peace of Your presence.

BRING IT HOME

How does trust play a role in a specific relationship where I feel loved?

Let's talk about who you trust first

DAY 2

"TRUST IN THE LORD
WITH ALL YOUR HEART…"
—PROVERBS 3:5, NLT

In week two, we talked about loving God with all our heart, mind, soul, and strength. Trusting God is no different. He calls us to trust Him with every part of ourselves, in every situation! Like we explored yesterday, you can't have love without trust.

When you feel deep love for someone else, it can be scary. Especially when it feels like you love them with all your heart. It is hard to imagine anything bad happening to them or them hurting your heart in some way. So, we start over-protecting our heart—shoving it in a triple-locked, fire-proof safe—afraid to fully trust even God. Because of hurt we've experienced in past relationships, we develop a "partial-trust" mindset when it comes to our intimacy with Jesus.

We "sort-of" trust Him, but we definitely have back-up plan A, B, C, and D—just in case God doesn't come through. We worry about imaginary scenarios of what might happen in our future, micromanage our closest relationships, and try to control everything and everyone. As soon as I sense myself doing this in ANY area of my life, it's a signal to me that I'm not fully trusting God—I've entered into the "partial-trust" zone.

The truth is: You can fully trust God. He will never ever leave you. He's not like our earthly relationships. He is eternal, and His love for you is greater than any love you will ever experience. You can place your entire trust in Him. He has a perfect plan for your life—one that will not disappoint.

Colossians 1:17 in the Amplified Version says, "And He Himself existed and is before all things, and in Him all things hold together. [His is the controlling, cohesive force of the universe.]" That's the God we are putting our trust in—One who knows everything, created everything, and sees your life from beginning to end. So, trusting God with all our heart starts by acknowledging that God is in control, and we are not.

Letting go is easier when we realize that God holds everything together, so nothing can fall apart. Romans 8:28 says, "God causes everything to work together for the good of those who love God." He is weaving everything together for a purpose you may not understand, but you can bet on this—it is good.

You can trust God with all your heart by believing what His Word says even when you feel differently or your circumstances are challenging.

PRAYER

God, You hold everything together. I trust that You, the One who created me, have great plans for my life. Please show me where I am trying to control and give me the grace to trust You more, even when it is hard!

BRING IT HOME

Where do I need to let go of control to embrace more of God?

"You give yourself too much credit if you think you can do something to remove God's love from you."

—BRENNA BLAIN

DAY 3

"TRUST IN THE LORD WITH ALL YOUR HEART, AND DO NOT LEAN ON YOUR OWN UNDERSTANDING."

—PROVERBS 3:5, ESV

Have you ever tried doing a trust fall with a friend? You know the type: you close your eyes, let go, and fall back, hoping they'll catch you? It's a total test of trust. At that moment, you are fully reliant on them to be there for you.

That's similar to what Proverbs 3:5 is talking about when it says, "lean not on your own understanding." The word **lean** describes resting one's weight on something for support. So, leaning on your own understanding quite literally means depending on yourself for support. God doesn't want us to do life alone. Instead, He wants to prop our arms up and guide our steps, partnering with us for every step of the journey.

Think of your own understanding—what you think is right or best—as a house of cards. It may stand up for a little bit, but with any resistance or wind, you can bet that it's going to topple over. Trusting in God, however, is like leaning on the sturdiest concrete building in the world. There's no risk of falling and hurting yourself.

In the Old Testament, the book of Numbers describes the Israelites' journey from Egypt—a land of intense slavery—to Canaan, their Promised Land. God repeatedly told the Israelites that He would lead them to this awesome land and give them victory over their enemies.

Before they entered Canaan, their leader, Moses, picked 12 people to scout out the land. They reported, "We entered the land you sent us to explore, and it is indeed a bountiful country—a land flowing with milk and honey ... But the people living there are powerful ... Let's choose a new leader and go back to Egypt!"⁸

Woah. Not only did God promise them an incredible new home, but they saw it with their own eyes! Still, only two of the 12 men who explored the land—Joshua and Caleb—were willing to move forward in faith. The other men responded according to their own understanding and made a decision out of fear. Because they trusted God, Caleb and Joshua's families were the only families out of the nation of Israel to enter into the Promised Land.

When you lean on your own understanding, you will receive less than God's best for your life. His plans and purposes for you are better than anything you could ask, imagine, or think.⁹ Simply trust Him.

PRAYER

God, I am sorry for all the times I've leaned on my own understanding or other people for support. Help me trust You even when it's scary or intimidating. Show me Your promises. I believe that Your plans for me are good!

BRING IT HOME

Who am I leaning on for support? Myself, others, or God?

Let's talk about who you trust first

DAY 4

"TRUST IN THE LORD WITH ALL YOUR HEART, AND LEAN NOT ON YOUR OWN UNDERSTANDING; **IN ALL YOUR WAYS ACKNOWLEDGE HIM…**"

—PROVERBS 3:5-6, NKJV

When you go on a walk or a hike, do you care more about the destination or the journey? Do you like to stop and smell the roses, or do you find ultimate satisfaction when you reach the summit? Good news—Proverbs 3:6 says that we can do both! We can enjoy the ride and reach a wonderful destination!

Let's unpack that verse a bit. The word **acknowledge** in Hebrew simply means to know, to learn, to perceive, discern, experience, confess, consider. To know someone in a way that you have a relationship with them, where you know them and they know you. In all your ways, throughout every path your life takes, you can know God. You can experience Him. You can learn to perceive Him throughout your day. You were made to have a rich relationship with Him, one where you can walk side by side and enjoy each other's presence.

Interestingly, Exodus 33:12-14 uses the same word for **ways** as "acknowledge" found in Proverbs 3:6. Check this out:

"One day Moses said to the Lord … 'If it is true that you look favorably on me, let me know your **ways** so I may understand you more fully and continue to enjoy your favor. And remember that this nation is your very own people.' The Lord replied, 'I will personally go with you, Moses, and I will give you rest—everything will be fine for you.'"

Moses was concerned about the journey of taking the Israelites to the Promised Land, so He asked for God to show Him the way. God's response? "I will personally go with you." Before God gave Moses a roadmap, He promised His presence.

I've heard it said that the center of God's will isn't a destination, it's a relationship. So often we concern ourselves with finding the right answer or making the perfect decision. We can get so wrapped up in where we are going that we forget Who we are going with.

Here's the truth: all you have to do is get into the presence of God, and He takes care of the details. How freeing is that?

PRAYER

God, thank You for Your presence. Help me trust You with the destination so I can enjoy the journey! I want to walk hand-in-hand with You and experience Your rest in every area of my life.

BRING IT HOME

What's the focus of my time with God—answers and outcomes or enjoying His presence? How can I rest in His presence today?

# DAY 5

"TRUST IN THE LORD WITH ALL YOUR HEART; DO NOT DEPEND ON YOUR OWN UNDERSTANDING. SEEK HIS WILL IN ALL YOU DO, **AND HE WILL SHOW YOU WHICH PATH TO TAKE.**"

—PROVERBS 3:5-6, NLT

It is normal to feel overwhelmed when you think about the future. There can be pressure to figure out who you are going to be, what you are going to do, and how you are going to get there. But guess what? **You don't have to have it all figured out right now.** That's straight from God's Word! The Bible makes it clear that God will walk beside you with a hand to hold and a compass to follow.

Here's how different Bible translations put the verse above:

- NIV: "He will **make** your paths straight."
- NLT: "He will **show** you which path to take."
- NKJV: "He shall **direct** your paths."

The original Hebrew word used here for **direct** means to make something straight, smooth, or pleasing. And **path** refers to a well-traveled road—like a lifestyle or the direction of your life.

This is the product of applying everything we've talked about this week! When you trust God fully, your life becomes clearer and easier to navigate. You will walk through life with confidence and purpose. Even when things get tough, God can smooth out the rough patches.

So, you don't need to know everything about tomorrow. Proverbs 16:9 says

"We can make our plans, but the Lord determines our steps." It's okay to make plans and prepare. However, trusting God involves holding those plans open-handedly and being okay when God reroutes you. His course always includes more love, peace, and joy than we can come up with on our own anyway!

Life with God is an adventure, and He wants to enjoy it with you. Will you accept His invitation into the unknown?

PRAYER

God, thank You for directing me when I feel lost or unsure. Please help me walk a path that pleases You. I want to walk with You on the journey, and I trust You to take me where I need to go!

BRING IT HOME

What are some things I am currently planning for? How can I start trusting God to direct my paths in those areas?

WILL YOU ACCEPT GOD'S INVITATION

into the unknown?

let's talk about

WHEN YOUR HEART HURTS

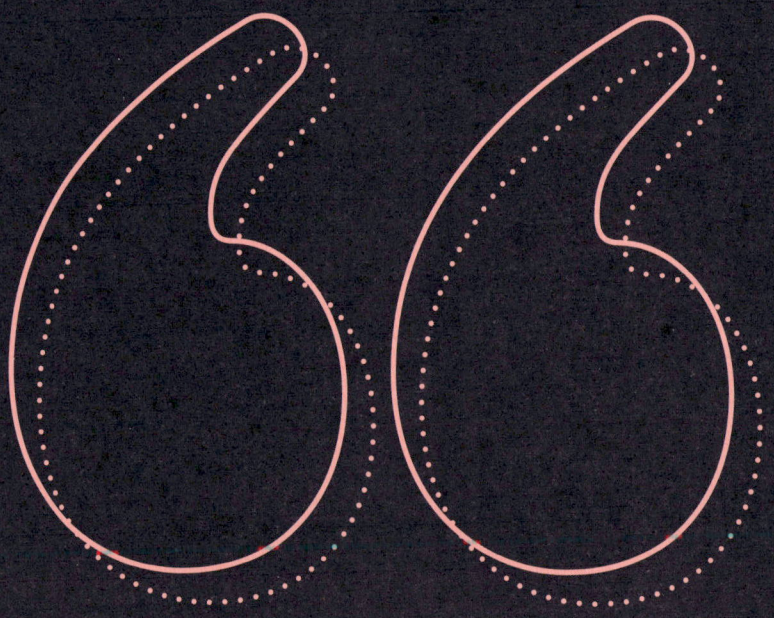

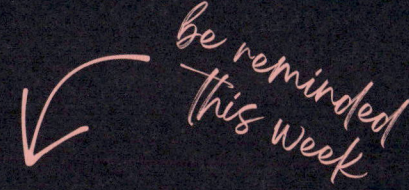

"The LORD is close to the brokenhearted; he rescues those whose spirits are crushed."

—Psalm 34:18, NLT

DAY 1

"THE LORD IS CLOSE TO THE BROKENHEARTED; HE RESCUES THOSE WHOSE SPIRITS ARE CRUSHED."

—PSALM 34:18, NLT

Though I haven't walked in your shoes for a day, a month, or a decade, I'm pretty certain you've walked through seasons where you have had a broken heart. Maybe someone has said something mean to you or a parent you thought would always be there has suddenly stepped out of your life for good. Your broken heart could be caused by a hard "no" from that team you really wanted to be a part of, the BFF you thought would be in your life forever, or a job you were really hoping to land.

Whatever the case, know that you aren't alone and that God cares about the small disappointments in your life as much as the big ones. Living fully loved means that God loves and cares for your broken heart, too.

This week, we are going to walk through Psalm 34:18 and talk through the kind of promises God has reserved for the **brokenhearted**. But first, let's talk about who wrote this beautiful passage.

This Psalm in particular was written by a man named David. He was one of the greatest kings in Israel and he loved God with all his heart—but that didn't exclude him from heartache. In fact, it often made his heart a target.

You see, David was anointed to be king at around 15 years old.[10] He was a normal kid who grew into a great man of God, but it seemed like even when he tried to do the right thing and live with integrity, he still got hurt. Do you ever feel that way? As if you're doing everything right, but you're still being treated unfairly? God sees those moments in your life.

You see, the King who was ruling during David's time—King Saul—was so jealous of David that he tried to kill him on multiple occasions, until eventually David had to run for his life. And now, instead of living in the palace, or with his family in his childhood home, David was forced to live in caves. Yes, dingy, hard, cold, wet, musty, dark caves. Everything he had once cherished was taken from him, and David's heart was broken many times during this season.

It was in this brokenhearted situation, with his life completely upended, that David wrote this Psalm. If anyone had a reason to be brokenhearted, it was David—but he also found a reason to hope in God. You can too.

Know this: When your heart is broken, God is ready to comfort it.

PRAYER

God, I know there are areas of my heart that have been broken in the past or are broken now. Help me to come to You with my broken heart because You love me.

BRING IT HOME

When was the last time someone else broke my heart?

DAY 2

"IF YOU **REPENT**, I WILL RESTORE YOU THAT YOU MAY SERVE ME..."

—JEREMIAH 15:19, NIV

There are times when people break my heart—but there are also times when I'm the one who does the breaking. I need no help from anyone else to feel remorse and regret when I've done something wrong. My heart usually feels crushed by what I've done.

It's in these times that I'm tempted to feel a truckload of shame. Why did I make that decision? I should have chosen better. I shouldn't have made that mean comment about a friend behind their back. I just shattered the trust I once had with that person. The list could go on forever.

In the Old Testament, the children of Israel made some pretty bad decisions. It seemed like year after year, their hearts kept breaking—and it was all their own doing! But God spoke a promise to Jeremiah in the middle of this heartbreak season: "If you repent, I will restore you..." I love that the Bible doesn't say that God casts us away when we mess up. No, the Bible says that He is ready to restore those who are repentant.

This word **repent** in the Bible means to change one's mind, to be grieved, to turn back towards God. It also means to carry back. You see, sometimes I'm the one who caused my heart to break because I chose to do things my way instead of God's way. It's in those moments that I have to come to God and "turn the other way." I have to tell Him I'm sorry, apologize to those I've hurt, and ask Him to help me change.

And you know what? God is right there with me—giving me courage to do the right thing and helping mend my heart in the process.

It's silly to believe that we will never make mistakes. Sometimes we don't need anyone else breaking our hearts because we have a sledgehammer ready to smash our own. Whether your heart is broken by someone else or by your own actions, know that God still welcomes you with open arms. Turn back to Him.

Your perfect performance does not determine God's level of love for you. He loves you as is, so you might as well turn back to Him and trust Him with your heart again.

Living fully loved means that He loves us in our brokenness too.

PRAYER

God, help heal my heart when I've done something wrong. I'm sorry for choosing to do things my way instead of Yours.

BRING IT HOME

When is the last time I broke my own heart with something I did?

LIVING FULLY LOVED MEANS THAT HE LOVES US IN OUR BROKENNESS TOO.

DAY 3

"HE **HEALS** THE BROKENHEARTED AND BANDAGES THEIR WOUNDS."

—PSALM 147:3, NLT

God attaches promises to your brokenhearted moments. This is a game-changer. It means that in the middle of our brokenhearted state, shattered pieces in hand, there is hope. We don't need to mend our broken hearts on our own—we can stand on the promises from God's Word.

Over the next three days, we are going to talk about three specific promises for the brokenhearted. I hope they breathe hope into your life and remind you that with God's help, your heart can and will beat again.

So, what does it mean to have a broken heart? The word **broken** in this verse is pretty intense. It doesn't just mean you have a little crack in your heart that is hardly noticeable. Instead, it means to burst, to break in pieces, to smash, to shatter, to completely crush or destroy. Basically, your once gorgeous heart now looks like blue raspberry Fun Dip.

When I feel like my heart is crushed, the first thing I want to do is hide and protect myself. Sometimes I don't even want people to know that my heart is broken because it makes me feel weak. I want to protect myself because I don't want others to crush my heart to an even greater degree. But this is no way to live.

God's first promise is this: He heals the brokenhearted. The word **heals** in Hebrew means to mend or cure, heal, recover, repair, thoroughly make whole. I love that this word means to thoroughly make whole. You may think there is no way that your heart will ever recover from being shattered, but God can do miracles in your life.

We can't heal our broken hearts, but God can. If we give our hearts to Him, He can heal us. He can do the impossible. He can teach us how to guard our hearts in the future by placing our hearts safely in His hands first. He can show us how to trust others and how to trust ourselves again.

Living fully loved gives us the right to take our hearts to Jesus and allow Him to start the healing process. He can do it—even when our hearts are shattered into a million pieces.

PRAYER

God, only you can really mend a broken heart. Remind me to bring my heart to You first for the healing I need.

BRING IT HOME

What are some other things I bring my heart to for healing rather than to God first?

let's talk about when your heart hurts

DAY 4

"THE LORD IS **CLOSE** TO THE BROKENHEARTED..."
—PSALM 34:18, NLT

I don't like feeling alone, especially when my heart is broken. I want someone to be right there with me. They might not always understand what I'm going through, but just their presence shows me how much they love me. Knowing that my loved ones won't leave me when life gets hard is something I cherish. I'm sure the same is true for you.

Friends that leave your life when it gets tough—when you've made an epic mistake or someone else has crushed your heart—only make the hurt go deeper. And yes, there are times and seasons where friends walk out of your life, but God is not that type of friend or father. He will never leave you.

God's second promise for the brokenhearted is one of His best—He is close to the brokenhearted. In this passage, the word **close** means near in place or time. An ally, someone you can count on for strength, close friend, or someone who walks alongside you. Sometimes, it's when my heart feels crushed that I sense God is the closest.

One of the most crushing moments of my life was when I lost my third child at 13 weeks pregnant. There was nothing I could do to save my baby. I prayed. I hoped. I asked God countless times for a miracle, but still I lost the baby and I felt shattered on the inside.

In the weeks to follow, I would make my way to our basement daily—weeping and waiting on the God I loved. I wanted to trust Him, even though I didn't understand why He would allow my heart to be broken this way. But the very God who allowed it was the One whose nearness carried me through it.

In those moments, I realized that I might not understand the "why" behind everything that happens in my life. It might not seem fair, but I can choose to release the details to God and wrap myself in the promise of His nearness, especially when my heart is broken. No words were necessary; just being with Him was what my broken heart needed.

When I spend time with Jesus in my brokenness, He reminds me of His love for me. It's being in His presence, close to Him, and receiving His love for us that we are healed.

PRAYER

God, thank You for being close to me when my heart is broken. Knowing that You care, even about my heartbreak, means a lot to me.

BRING IT HOME

How does it help knowing that God is close to me when my heart is broken?

God, thank You for being *close* to me when my heart is broken 💔

# DAY 5

"THE LORD IS NEAR TO THE HEARTBROKEN AND HE **SAVES** THOSE WHO ARE CRUSHED IN SPIRIT (CONTRITE IN HEART, TRULY SORRY FOR THEIR SIN)."

—PSALM 34:18, AMP

I can't express how excited I am for this last day of the week with you. We are going to talk about the third promise God has reserved for the brokenhearted. And let me tell you, when I started studying this promise, my heart jumped on the inside of me—it's just that good!

First promise—God **heals** the brokenhearted. Second promise—He is **close** to the brokenhearted. Third promise—He **saves** the brokenhearted.

Get ready for your mind to be blown, because the word "saves" in Hebrew will literally transform your life if you can understand its meaning.

Saves is an action word meaning to **save, help, deliver,** and **defend**. The underlying idea is to **bring you to a place of safety**. It conveys the idea of **deliverance** from tribulation, **rescue** from your enemies, **victory** in time of war, the **protective duty** of a shepherd over his flock, **avenging wrongs**, and giving **compassionate aid** to you in your time of need. It's the **salvation** that only comes from God.

Not only is God going to heal your broken heart and draw close to you, but the Bible says He saves you. He will help you, deliver you, and defend you behind the scenes. He will bring you and your heart to a safe place. He will rescue you, protect you, help you, and have compassion on you. Basically, God will save you in a way that only He can.

When our hearts are broken, we might be tempted to go to other things that offer a temporary band-aid for our condition. The Bible is clear; the only person that can heal your broken heart is God. Would you bring it to Him and trust that He will save you in ways that no one else can?

Living fully loved is knowing that God has the power to heal and save the most precious part of us—our hearts.

PRAYER

God, thank You for saving me. You provide for me. You protect me and comfort me, especially when my heart is broken.

BRING IT HOME

How does knowing the promise that God will save me change my perspective on heartbreak?

let's talk about

BEING FILLED WITH PEACE

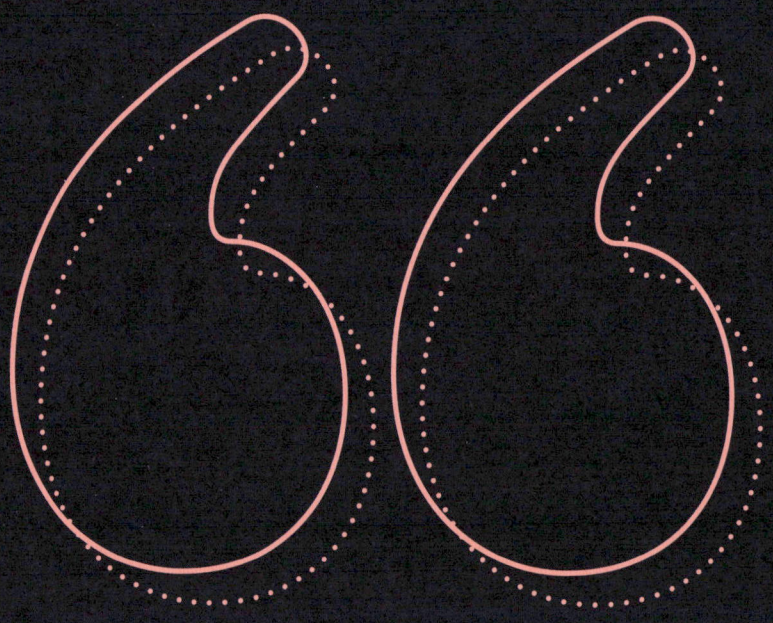

Be anxious for nothing, but in everything by prayer and supplication, with thanksgiving, let your requests be made known to God; and the peace of God, which surpasses all understanding, will guard your hearts and minds through Christ Jesus."

–Philippians 4:6-7, NKJV

meditate on this week

DAY 1

"DON'T WORRY ABOUT ANYTHING; INSTEAD, PRAY ABOUT EVERYTHING. TELL GOD WHAT YOU NEED, AND THANK HIM FOR ALL HE HAS DONE. THEN YOU WILL EXPERIENCE GOD'S PEACE..."

—PHILIPPIANS 4:6-7, NLT

In a world where there is so much you could worry about, the Word of God promises perfect peace. You don't have to worry about anything—not your health, what people think about you, your family, or your future. That's a crazy different approach from the anxious age we live in today! As a fully loved daughter of God, you are meant to experience **complete freedom** in your heart and mind.

The Apostle Paul wrote Philippians 4:6-7 while imprisoned in a dark, musty cell in Rome. Unsure of what the future held—freedom, execution, or another day of cold and hunger—Paul was still able to experience God's peace in his heart. This divine exchange is available to you as well. You can give God your worry, and He will give you peace in its place. That's a pretty great trade!

Here's how it works. Whenever you start to worry, you can draw on this simple process: pray, tell God what you need, and give thanks. Then, God's peace will guard your heart. Remember our verse in week one, Proverbs 4:23: "Guard your heart above all else, for it determines the course of your life."

Philippians 4:6-7 is the blueprint for HOW you can start to guard your heart with the power of God's peace. In this passage, the Greek word for **guard** translates to "protect by a military guard to prevent hostile invasion." That's such a good picture of what worry and anxiety can feel like: a hostile invasion.

Note that you are not responsible for being this strong, militant force. In His goodness, God wants to guard your heart from any foreign enemy that wants to invade it.

As Christians, we don't muster up peace on our own—we get to sit at the table with the Prince of Peace and receive it from Him. The peace that Paul describes in this passage is more than just a tranquil feeling. It exceeds all understanding, is available in any circumstance, and transforms any atmosphere. The Greek word for **peace** is connected to another word meaning "to weave together."[11] God's peace brings harmony, weaving together our relationships with others, ourselves, and God.

Living fully loved means you have a promise from God for peace. He wants to bring peace to any area of unrest in your heart and relationships—to weave everything together with His goodness and grace. Throughout the rest of the week, we will dive deeper into how to trust God so you can receive this incredible gift!

PRAYER

God, I understand that inviting Your peace into my heart starts with recognizing the things that try to steal it. Help me recognize the things that try to steal my peace and trust You in the process.

BRING IT HOME

What worries do I need to exchange for God's peace?

DAY 2

> "DON'T WORRY ABOUT ANYTHING, BUT IN EVERYTHING, **THROUGH PRAYER** AND PETITION WITH THANKSGIVING, PRESENT YOUR REQUESTS TO GOD."
>
> —PHILIPPIANS 4:6, CSV

Where do you notice worry first? Is it buzzing in the back of your brain? A sinking feeling in your gut? A lump rising in your throat? Or a heavy weight on your chest? Whatever the warning signs, take them as a yellow caution light telling you to slow down, pause, and pray.

This is easier said than done. If you're like me, the root of anxiousness is a core belief of "not enough." Not enough energy. Not enough resources. Not enough strength. Not enough confidence. And certainly not enough time. Can I be honest? When worry hits me, the first thing I want to do is drive really fast through every red light. Often, I don't want to pause and look to God because that takes too much time.

The second thing I want to do is control. I try to order all the things that feel in disarray and cram the chaos into tidy, neat boxes. At the end of the day, this is a recipe for more worry. Control compounds until we fall into the illusion of thinking we are in charge. That's a really heavy weight to bear, but here's the good news: you don't have to carry it! We are not our source; God is our source. **We don't achieve peace; we receive peace.**

Worry makes life seem cloudy, confusing, and complicated. God's peace brings clarity, and the route to it is simple: "Don't worry about anything, instead pray about everything." This is the kind of life God has in store for us. As we trust Him with our hearts and learn to receive His love, a newfound peace and clarity is ours for the taking.

The Bible doesn't give us any slack here. We are commanded to relentlessly attack worry in all areas. From your dreams to what you are eating for dinner, God cares about it all. Living loved means that the Holy Spirit will help us recognize that God wants to bring His peace into every moment.

Worry doesn't have to send you into a spiral of doom and gloom. Instead, it can be a sweet invitation to enter into God's presence and trust Him with every detail.

PRAYER

God, sometimes I let worry take over my life. Help me identify it and then give it to You. Help me to learn to trust You with every detail.

BRING IT HOME

What do I normally do when I feel worried? How can I start to turn to God first?

Christ alone

CAN BRING
LASTING PEACE

PEACE WITH GOD
PEACE AMONG NATIONS

and peace within our hearts

—BILLY GRAHAM

wk.6 DAY 3

"... BUT IN EVERYTHING BY PRAYER AND **SUPPLICATION**, WITH THANKSGIVING, LET YOUR REQUESTS BE MADE KNOWN TO GOD;"
—PHILIPPIANS 4:6, NKJV

Sometimes we overcomplicate our relationship with God. Have you ever been at a loss of what to pray about? Philippians 4:6 makes it really clear and simple. You can always pray about what you want, what you need, and what you are grateful for. God cares about it all.

Sounds too good to be true? It kind of is. But it's not—it's true! It's like you have a BFF on speed dial who will always answer your call, day or night. It's being a fully loved daughter with a Father who loves you with an amazing agape love, who cares about every detail of your life and has your best interest at heart—always.

And trust me, God makes it plain in the Bible that He cares about every part of your life, and He loves doing good on your behalf. He just loves you that much. It's part of the promised package deal of living fully loved. Psalm 37:23 says: "God directs the steps of the godly. He delights in every detail of their lives."[12] And Psalm 84:11 tells us: "The Lord will withhold no good thing from those who do what is right."

It brings God joy to delight in the details of your life, to fulfill your simplest desires and your deepest longings. However, He can't grant a request you don't make! James 4:2 says: "you don't have what you want because you don't ask God for it." Philippians 4:6 instructs us to make our requests known to God through prayer and supplication. The original Greek word that Paul uses for **supplication** is a noun that means the expression of a need or desire, to petition for oneself.

Throughout the scriptures, supplication rarely describes a tangible need like food or water. More often than not, a supplication conveys a deep desire and longing of the heart. Zacharias made supplication for a child in his old age. The apostle Paul made supplication for the people of Israel to be saved. Similarly, you are invited to lay your biggest dreams, deepest needs, and most vulnerable moments before the heart of God.

You are not too much for Him, and He will not disappoint you!

PRAYER

God, help me to trust You with every part of my life. I know that our relationship needs to be built on trust, so help me to be open and honest with You.

BRING IT HOME

What are some of the things I am longing for in this season?

DAY 4

"TELL GOD WHAT YOU NEED, AND **THANK HIM** FOR ALL HE HAS DONE."
—PHILIPPIANS 4:6, NLT

Gratitude is one of those things that is a natural byproduct of living fully loved. When you and I understand how loved we are by God, receive His love daily, and allow our hearts to rest safely in His hands, we can't help but be grateful. You see, God loves it when you show Him you love Him, but He loves hearing it too.

Did you know that it's impossible to be worried and grateful at the same time? Anxiousness can send you into a spiral of fearful "what ifs," but gratitude reminds you of what's real. I often say it this way: Gratitude is the gateway to reality. And, as Philippians 4:6 shows us, it's also a gateway to peace!

King David shows us this truth throughout Psalm 103:1-8, with the first two verses saying: "Let all that I am praise the Lord; with my whole heart, I will praise his holy name. Let all that I am praise the Lord; may I never forget the good things he does for me."

Then, David continues to list what God does for him—"He forgives all my sins and heals all my diseases"— and qualities that he loves about Him—He's "slow to get angry and filled with unfailing love."

In this Psalm, David is doing one of my favorite practices to do when I feel worried: making a gratitude list. I encourage you to try it out! Make a list of what you are grateful for, and watch your worry fade in the process.

You may start with something as simple as "God, thank You for sunshine" or "Thank You for Starbucks iced lattes." However, as you keep going, you will undoubtedly uncover a deeper thankfulness for what God is doing in your life. Maybe it's "God, thank You for always being there for me" or "Thank You for how You are moving in my family."

Every piece of gratitude you include on your list is an anchor to the overwhelming truth: God is faithful, and you can trust Him with your heart. As you reflect on how God has already moved in your life, your confidence in His plans and provision for your future will grow. In that, you can rest and have peace!

Let gratitude be a pathway to the peace promised to you.

PRAYER

God, I'm starting now by saying thank You. Thank You for taking care of me, for loving me, for protecting my heart, and for the amazingly good God You are.

BRING IT HOME

What am I grateful for? Today I will make a list and keep writing until I can't think of anything else!

GRATITUDE ---> **IS**

THE ---> **GATEWAY**

TO ---> **PEACE.**

DAY 5

"WHATEVER THINGS ARE TRUE ... NOBLE ... JUST ... PURE ... LOVELY ... OF GOOD REPORT, IF THERE IS ANY VIRTUE AND IF THERE IS ANYTHING PRAISEWORTHY— MEDITATE ON THESE THINGS."

—PHILIPPIANS 4:8, NKJV

God has blessed us with incredible minds. They can solve complex problems, carry meaningful conversations, tell captivating stories, and appreciate beauty. The average person has around 70,000 thoughts per day (that's 50 per minute!)[13] Yet, not all of these thoughts work for our good.

In the past decade, psychologists and researchers have been studying Automatic Negative Thoughts. Harvard Health Publishing describes ANTs as all-or-nothing ideas that "leave us stuck in good or bad, success or failure, with no middle ground between the two extremes. If you've fallen short, it's because you're completely incompetent – or so the thinking goes."[14]

When we experience stressful situations or painful events, our brains can jump to the worst-case scenario. Often, we are quick to think mean things about ourselves that directly oppose God's thoughts about us.

Philippians 4:8 offers a different solution, encouraging us to meditate on things that are true, noble, just, pure, lovely, of good report, virtuous, and praiseworthy. These kinds of thoughts are the result of a mind and heart guarded by God's peace! Whatever you think about will come out in your streams of life and affect your ability to encourage others. So, if you want to offer true, lovely, and praiseworthy things to yourself, family, and friends, it starts with your thought life. Remember, your heart and mind are connected.

In the weeks to come, know that you don't have to entertain every thought that comes into your head. You have complete control over what you think about. Ask the Holy Spirit to help you live loved in your heart and mind by meditating on what God says is good and true.

A practical way to take your thoughts captive is to keep a "negative thought tracker" for a week. You can write in your journal or make a note on your phone. Every time you recognize a fearful or self-deprecating thought, write it down. Then, replace the lie with truth from the Word of God. Over time, you will recognize common thought traps and be able to choose truth more readily.

PRAYER

God, help me take control of negative thoughts that race through my brain about myself and others. Help me choose Your thoughts for my life instead.

BRING IT HOME

What one negative thought I have about myself on a regular basis and how can I align that thought with God's Word instead?

let's talk about being filled with peace

let's talk about

YOUR DEEPEST DESIRES

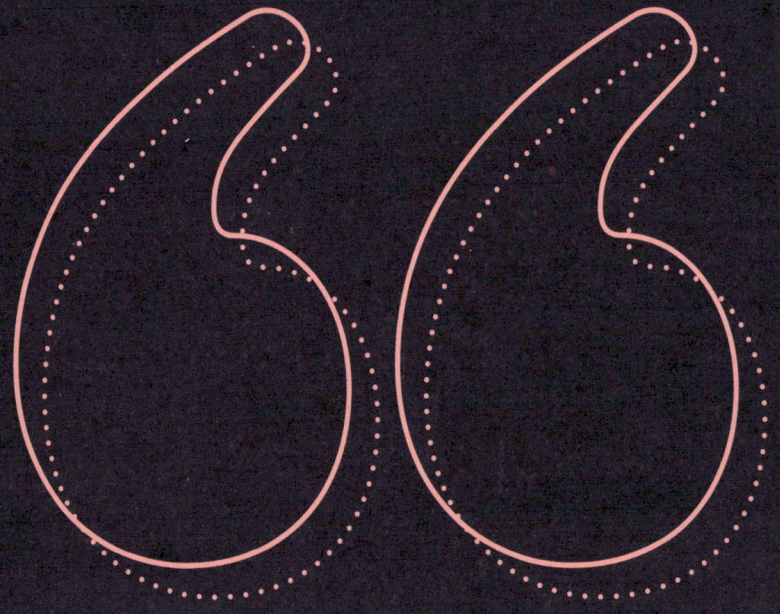

practice this week

"Delight yourself also in the Lord and He shall give you the desires of your heart."

—Proverbs 37:4, NKJV

DAY 1

"WHEREVER YOUR **TREASURE** IS, THERE THE DESIRES OF YOUR HEART WILL BE ALSO."

—MATTHEW 6:21, NLT

Before we talk about your deepest desires, let's talk about what you treasure, because what you treasure affects your desires and your heart. Have you ever asked yourself what you treasure most in life? Really think about it. It could be a number of things: Your family. Friendships. Having those sweet Jordans to wear every day. Maybe you treasure social media. How many likes you have on Instagram. How "opened" you are on Snap, or how many followers you have on YouTube or TikTok.

Or maybe for you it's all about status and having or being the best. Being an A+ student. Being the best athlete you can be. Having the most gorgeous friends. Dating the cutest, most popular guy you know. Using the best new hair products or skin care—Summer Fridays, Bubble, and Sol de Janeiro—and posting about it, of course.

The Bible is clear: our heart can't be in two different places. What you treasure most is where you'll find your heart.

The word **treasure** means something of great worth or value.[15] It's wealth stored up or hoarded. It's that thing a pirate devotes his life to finding. Sailing, buried-treasure-map in hand—navigating tempests and trials in hopes of discovering the secret treasure that will make all his dreams come true. He gives his life to it because it's the thing he treasures most.

Now, Jesus isn't saying that we can't treasure having nice things. He isn't saying that we can't pursue great friends or relationships in life, that we can't try our best academically or be on social media. What He's asking is what you treasure **most** in life.

Think about what you long for most. What you treasure above all else. It's what you devote your time, energy, and thoughts towards. Be honest. It's ok if it's not God. He's not mad about it. He loves it when you are honest with Him. But maybe, if it's not God, you can start asking Him to help you make Him your number one treasure.

PRAYER

God, I'm not sure You are my number one treasure in life, but I'd like for You to be. Help me to treasure You above all other things.

BRING IT HOME

What do I spend most of my time doing or thinking about?

# wk.7 DAY 2

> **"STOCKPILE TREASURE IN HEAVEN,** WHERE IT'S SAFE FROM MOTH AND RUST AND BURGLARS. IT'S OBVIOUS, ISN'T IT? THE PLACE WHERE YOUR TREASURE IS, IS THE PLACE YOU WILL MOST WANT TO BE, AND END UP BEING."
>
> —MATTHEW 6:21, MSG

I can't speak for you, but I know that sometimes I think I need material things to feel secure and cared for. I need just enough money in my bank account. I need to have 3.5 best friends. I need to have a decent car, a roof over my head—and oh yeah, the newest iPhone to feel as if I'm doing good. Living in a consumer culture, we unknowingly live with the fear of being canceled if we don't have more of the right things.

In a study done in the 1990's, when Americans were asked how much money they would need to live the American dream, they basically said double what they currently make. If they made $25,000, they said they would need $50,000. If they made $100,000, they said they would need $200,000.[16]

What does that show you? It shows me that no matter what we currently have—when it comes to material, earthly treasure—our tendency is to always crave more, to never be satisfied.

God knew that the world's material things would be temporary and couldn't fulfill the deep need within our hearts for Him. Of course they won't satisfy us! No wonder we keep wanting more. That's why He tells us flat-out: treasure here on earth will someday vanish, but treasure in heaven—where God resides—will never pass away.

If you never feel like you're happy or fulfilled, it's time to examine your heart. Could it be that you feel that way because you treasure something here on earth greater than you treasure Jesus?

Living fully loved helps you enjoy the material things in life, because you know that your ultimate treasure and fulfillment isn't found in those things. You live knowing there is one thing that was created to satisfy you on the inside—only one thing you were meant to treasure most. It's a relationship with Jesus—and you've got that, so you can already be fulfilled!

PRAYER

God, when I'm tempted to treasure other things above You, remind me what I was created for and that only You can satisfy.

BRING IT HOME

How can I start to live like God is my greatest treasure?

wk.7 DAY 3

"GODLINESS WITH CONTENTMENT IS GREAT GAIN."

—1 TIMOTHY 6:6, NKJV

By now, we know that we should treasure Jesus above all else and enjoy Him more than anything else. But just because we want Jesus to be our treasure doesn't mean that the world around us doesn't fight like crazy for our hearts. Lord knows it does, and oftentimes Jesus starts slipping out of His position as our main priority. Let me put it this way: Jesus may have been our main treasure a few summers ago, but now He's slipped back into 15th place—right below dish duty.

So how do we keep Jesus as number one in our lives? How do we treasure the heavenly things more than the material things of earth? We need the Holy Spirit's help, and we need to realize that part of the battle is won through contentment.

1 Timothy 6:6 is going to be a game-changer in our treasure study. According to this verse, there are two ingredients to living in a state of "great gain" or true fulfillment (i.e., a state of being fully loved): godliness and contentment.

The word **godliness** just means that we are reverent towards God. It also means spontaneous feelings of the heart toward Him. Basically, we are living a life that reveres Him above all else. But that's not all that's needed to live an abundant life. We also need contentment.

Contentment is such a rich word. It means satisfaction and sufficiency—meaning you carry a happiness that is not dependent on "things," but on God's will and His plan for your life. You let go of the need to always have more—

which, for the western world, seems counter-cultural. To live fully loved, we must embrace the truth that more doesn't always make us happy.

I think contentment is a superpower—and not many people possess it. When you do have it, it transforms your life and the lives of those around you.

It's saying, "God, I'm satisfied with what You've given me. You are sufficient. I'm happy with what I have. I have food on the table. I have clothes on my back. I have family and friends who love me. I have a God that is for me and has great plans for my life. I want You to know that is enough."

PRAYER

God, help me make the prayer above my prayer. Help me live like You are always enough.

BRING IT HOME

In what areas of my life am I most discontent? Why?

contentment

1. Practice gratitude. When we are grateful, we enjoy what we currently have instead of always wanting more. Something in our heart changes towards God and towards others as we practice gratitude daily.

2. Be present. When you're with someone—be fully there! Put down your phone and pay attention. Practice listening more than you speak. Try to understand others.

3. Enjoy the little things. A cup of hot chocolate with extra-large marshmallows. A car ride to the beach with friends. A blue raspberry slushy from the gas station. There's joy to be found in the everydayness of life. Ask God to give you eyes to see it.

4. Stop comparing. Theodore Roosevelt said, "Comparison is the thief of joy." And guess what? Social media can bring comparison into our lives when we least expect it. Limit your time on social media. Control who you follow. Follow people who encourage your heart towards God. Unfollow people who make you constantly feel dissatisfied with life.

5. Start replacing. Replace your cravings for more stuff with truth from God's Word. Remind yourself daily that He is for you (Psalm 56:9), that He loves you no matter what you do (Romans 5:8), and that He is more than enough for everything you need (2 Corinthians 9:8-11).

DAY 4

"TAKE **DELIGHT** IN THE LORD, AND HE WILL GIVE YOU YOUR HEART'S DESIRES."

—PSALM 34:8, NLT

Let's dig into the verse we are meditating on this week. If there was ever a verse I loved clinging to as a kid, it was this one. How do I get what I want? Well, the Bible says that if I delight in the Lord, He will give me what my heart desires. That is like the BEST PROMISE EVER!

As an 8-year-old kid, my heart had a lot of desires: a new pony for Christmas, five puppies under the tree, and a new baby doll. As a teenage girl, the desires of my heart were more along the lines of being in the most popular friend group, dating that happily-ever-after guy, getting a new Jeep Wrangler, and growing up to own a white house with a picket fence.

So as a kid, I thought this verse was my ticket to getting everything I wanted! But that's not what this verse means—at least not entirely. Psalm 34:8 is as much about the transformation of our hearts as it is about our heart's desires. Here's how it works.

First, we need to delight in the LORD. The word **delight** in Hebrew means to be soft or pliable, or have delight. Right away, with this definition I'm asking myself: Am I pliable, moldable, soft in the hands of God?

Another meaning of this word is to take a high degree of gratification or pleasure in. To be extremely satisfied. To enjoy immensely. **So now I'm asking myself: Am I extremely satisfied in my relationship with God?** Do I actually enjoy being with Him—spending time in His Word and prayer, inviting Him to join me in my day?[17]

The more time I spend with Him—the more I get to know God through His Word, and the more open and vulnerable I am with Him in prayer, sharing what is really going on in my life—the more satisfied I am in my relationship with Him. And then, guess what? The things I want change. My heart changes in His presence. The things I used to value and think I needed just don't seem that important anymore.

So yes, delight yourself in the LORD and He will give you your heart's desires—but as you delight, your desires change. You release what you think is best for you and start to embrace only God's best for your life.

And if you don't enjoy being with Jesus—fully-loved-daughter—that's ok too. Talk to Him about it. He loves to hear that you want His help to start enjoying your relationship with Him. He can help you love being with Him.

PRAYER

God, I want to be honest—I don't always delight in You first. Help show me how to delight in my relationship with You. You have my heart.

BRING IT HOME

Do I find joy or delight in my relationship with God? Why or why not?

wk.7 DAY 5

"TASTE AND SEE THAT THE LORD IS GOOD; BLESSED IS THE MAN WHO TRUSTS IN HIM!"
—PSALM 37:8, NKJV

One of my favorite desserts is a hot fudge brownie sundae. The brownie must be baked to perfection, with Guittard milk chocolate chips on the inside and extra chewy edges on the outside—then topped with Kinder Bueno italian ice cream and crumbled Reese's peanut butter cups. If I had never tasted that sundae, I wouldn't crave it. But because I've tasted it—and experienced its gooey-delectableness—just describing it makes my mouth water.

In my experience, my relationship with God is a lot like developing a taste for that hot fudge brownie sundae. The more I taste it, the more I know how good it tastes, and the more I crave it.

Psalm 37:8 says to taste and see that God is good. To **taste** means to test the flavor of something by taking a small part of it into your mouth. So the more you taste of God and His Word, the more you will see that He is good. It's like you develop a flavor pallet for Him. His goodness is something you'll start to realize you can't live without.

The word **good** in this verse means something that is well-pleasing, fruitful, or morally correct. It's described as appealing and pleasant to the senses, useful and profitable, abundant and plentiful, kind and benevolent. "Good" is a state of well-being or happiness, better than any alternative.

God is far better than anything else you could experience in life. He brings kindness and well-being into your heart. He is pleasant, abundant, and oh-so good.

My challenge to you is to taste and see for yourself that He is good. Maybe you have heard about His goodness from others, but you haven't tasted Him consistently enough to discover that His goodness is meant for you.

Living fully loved gives us all access to a really good God who doesn't disappoint—He only gets better with time. Develop your spiritual taste buds for Him by consistently spending time with Him. Dig into His Word this week. Share your hopes and dreams and challenges with Him through prayer. Inevitably, you will discover that His goodness isn't just for others; it's for you!

PRAYER

God, thank You for Your goodness. Help me to develop a spiritual appetite for You, where I begin to crave You above anything else in my life.

BRING IT HOME

With the Holy Spirit's help, how can I start to develop a hunger for God?

that the Lord is good

—Psalm 37:8

let's talk about

WHAT COMES OUT OF YOUR HEART

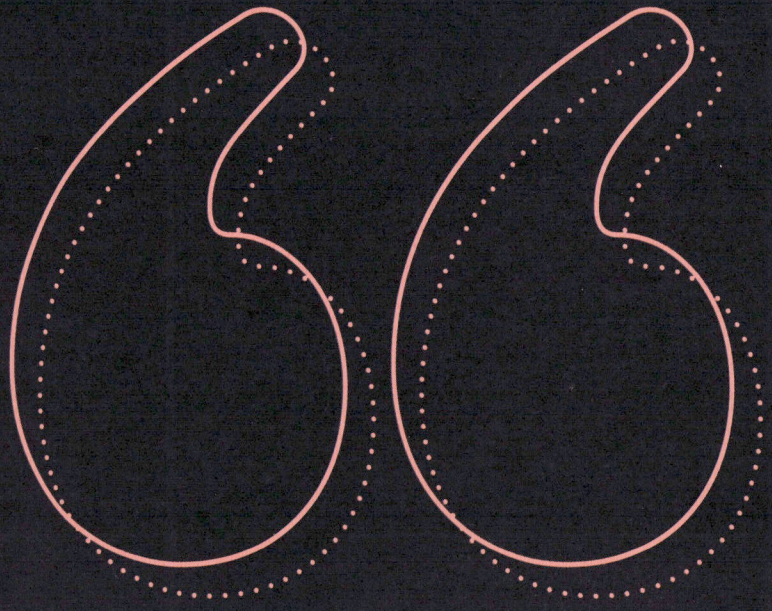

verse to meditate on

"It's not what goes into your body that defiles you; you are defiled by what comes from your heart."

—Mark 7:15, NLT

DAY 1

"IT'S NOT WHAT GOES INTO YOUR BODY THAT DEFILES YOU; **YOU ARE DEFILED BY WHAT COMES FROM YOUR HEART.**"

—MARK 7:15, NLT

For the past seven weeks, we've been studying God's Word—digging deep in our hearts and learning how to live fully loved from the inside out. For this last week, we are going to talk about what to do from here. How can you give yourself a "heart check" in the weeks, months, years, and decades to come? How can you live fully loved for the rest of your life? Thankfully, the Holy Spirit will help us, and God's Word gives us clarity on how to check our hearts.

We are going to focus on Mark 7 for this last week, where Jesus tells us that it's not what we put in us that defiles us, but rather what comes out of us that reveals the condition of our hearts. **Let's be clear: God is not interested in the filtered version of you.** He wants the real you—the open, vulnerable you with your heart on the table. The you who ugly cries with makeup running down your face, the you that you want to hide—yeah, He wants that you.

In Jesus' day, the Jews created hundreds of purity laws in addition to the laws given by God in the first five books of the Old Testament. They did everything they could to look right on the outside in the sight of God and man, but God saw inside their hearts.

The Pharisees thought their manmade laws were keeping them from being like the average sinner, but Jesus flipped their expectations upside down. In Matthew 23:23, Jesus reprimands the religious leaders and says: "What sorrow awaits you teachers of religious law and you Pharisees. Hypocrites! For you are careful to tithe even the tiniest income from your herb gardens, but you ignore the more important aspects of the law—justice, mercy, and faith. You should tithe, yes, but do not neglect the more important things."[18] They looked like they were doing everything right, but their hearts were in the wrong place.

God's chosen people—the people He has set apart—are identified by their hearts, not what's on the outside. Remember, our hearts are who we are on the inside—our minds, feelings, emotions, and intellect. **Heart check:** It doesn't matter if you do all the right things on the outside if the "why" or motive behind them isn't right. Our heart affects everything else in our lives. Jesus calls us to pay attention to what's happening on the inside, not just what we show on the outside. But here's the amazing news: We don't have to clean up our hearts on our own! God is ready to do a "heart check" and give us a clean, new heart—if we're willing to let Him.

PRAYER

God, I realize the importance of my heart. As I'm giving my heart to You, help what flows out of it to be good in Your eyes.

BRING IT HOME

Are there any parts of my life where I feel more focused on how things look on the outside instead of what's going on inside? How can I invite God to help me change that?

let's talk about what comes out of your heart

DAY 2

"YOU HAVE LET GO OF THE COMMANDS OF GOD AND ARE **HOLDING ON TO HUMAN TRADITIONS**."

—MARK 7:8, NIV

Throughout this final week, we are doing a heart check and reminding ourselves that what comes out of us reveals what is in us. Over the next few days, we are going to dive into outward symptoms of a heart that isn't quite aligned with the living loved life God has called us to.

One of the first things that come out of my heart when my heart is a little off is **perfectionism**. For me, perfectionism shows itself when I prioritize rules, regulations, and my performance above an intimate relationship with God. A God who loves ALL of me, by the way, even the imperfect parts.

For all of Jesus' lifetime, Israel was under Roman rule. Many Jews believed that if they were obedient enough to the scriptures, the Messiah would come save them, and they could rule their own nation again.

Here's the problem: Many Jewish leaders during Jesus' time cared more about the religious teachers' interpretation of scripture than what the scriptures actually said! Then, they held others to impossible standards and judged them harshly when they failed to meet the requirements they had created—not God. In Mark 7, this was the context Jesus found Himself in when Jewish leaders asked Him, "Why don't your disciples follow our age-old tradition? They eat without first performing the hand washing ceremony."

To that, Jesus responded: "Isaiah was right when he prophesied about you hypocrites; as it is written: 'These people honor me with their lips, but their hearts are far from me. They worship me in vain; their teachings are merely human rules.' You have let go of the commands of God and are holding on to human traditions."

The same is true for us. Our religious traditions don't mean anything to God if our hearts are far from Him. You don't need to read your Bible or listen to worship music just so you can check a box off your to-do list. He wants your heart.

Heart check: Let's ask the Holy Spirit to show us the difference between biblical truth and personal perfectionism. Like the Pharisees, we can be tempted to interpret God's Word to suit our personal agenda and turn it into a performance. Here's the irony—many of the Jews in Jesus' day were so wrapped up in their traditions and opinions that they missed the Messiah they were working so hard to meet!

PRAYER

God, I don't want to be so wrapped up in my to-do list for You that I miss actually giving You my heart. Help me to focus on our relationship over my accomplishments every day.

BRING IT HOME

Does my time with God feel more like a relationship or a list of religious requirements?

Let's talk about what comes out of your heart

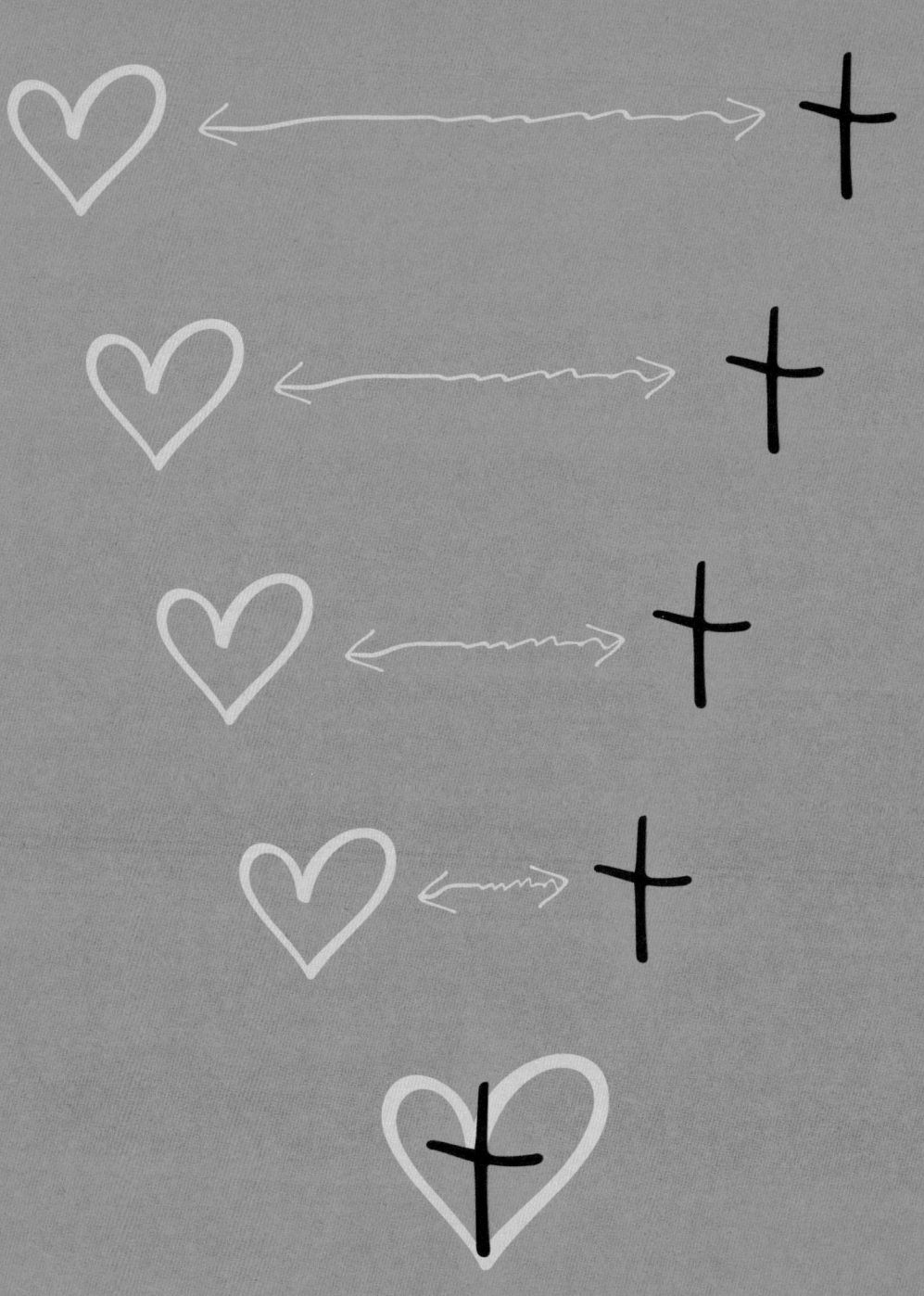

< Our religious traditions don't mean anything to God if our hearts are far from Him.

< Relationship first.

DAY 3

THEY BEGGED HIM TO LET THE SICK TOUCH AT LEAST THE FRINGE OF HIS ROBE, AND ALL WHO TOUCHED HIM WERE HEALED."

—MARK 6:56, NLT

You can learn a lot about a passage of scripture by paying attention to the stories that surround it. Just like reading a book, one chapter builds upon another, and their interrelationships can highlight different truths.

So, let's rewind to the chapter before the Mark 7:1-19 passage we have been unpacking this week. When Jesus visited the town of Gennesaret, Mark 6:56 tells us that "Wherever he went—in villages, cities, or the countryside—they brought the sick out to the marketplaces. They begged him to let the sick touch at least the fringe of his robe, and all who touched him were healed."

During this time, sick people were often outcast from society. They were regarded as unclean or sinners, as if God was punishing them for their wrongdoings by making them ill. "Righteous" people often avoided interacting with them, and they certainly avoided touching them. Their impurity might be contagious, after all! The last thing people would have expected was for the Son of God to welcome, heal, and accept them on such an intimate level.

When my heart isn't in its 'fully loved' state with God, I don't live like the Jesus in this passage. Instead, **pride** seeps into everything I do. Not the good kind of pride either; it's the self-promoting, "I'm better than you" type of pride. It's a pride full of arrogance and presuming to be better than others.

Pride shows itself in many ways in my life. Sometimes I start pridefully protecting my world against people I think are somehow "less than" or

unworthy to be around me. I'll start to exclude people I think may somehow contaminate my image. I'll use excuses like "show me your friends and I'll show you your future" to justify being unloving towards others. I start to think the worst about others, crafting their faults into a list a mile long—while imagining my own could fit into a tiny paragraph.

When my heart is right with God, it's like my dark, prideful sunglasses are taken off and I can love deeply. I stop worrying about myself long enough to see each person around me as loved and valuable in God's eyes. Pride vanishes, and humility takes its place.

Heart check: Pride can be sneaky, but once the Holy Spirit helps us identify it, we can ask God to help us walk in loving humility before Him and others.

PRAYER

God, I know I can be prideful at times. Help bring my heart back on track to live in loving humility with You. I need Your help every step of the way.

BRING IT HOME

What areas of my life do I sometimes see pride showing itself?

Let's talk about what comes out of your heart

DAY 4

"WOMAN, YOU HAVE **GREAT FAITH**! YOUR REQUEST IS GRANTED."

—MATTHEW 15:28, NLT

Your faith is precious to God, and it has power. When my heart isn't in alignment with Him, another thing that comes out of me is **unbelief**. I start to trust that my way is better than God's way. I don't believe that He has my best interest at heart. I've given my heart to too many other things and it's been broken too many times. I begin to doubt His goodness and even His love for me.

Today, we're looking at a powerful example of what happens when faith leads the way instead of unbelief. Right after Jesus speaks about the heart in Mark 7:1-19, something interesting happens in verses 24-29. Jesus travels to a place called Tyre and Sidon, a region where Gentiles (people who weren't Jewish) lived. At the time, Jews and Gentiles didn't mix much. A faithful Jew would not step foot into a Gentile's home. But Jesus wasn't following those cultural rules—He had a mission to show that God's love is for everyone.

When Jesus arrives, a Greek Gentile woman comes to Him in desperation. She has a daughter that only Jesus can heal and she's determined to get help, but Jesus' first response is surprising. He says, "First I should feed the children—my own family, the Jews. It isn't right to take food from the children and throw it to the dogs." Wait—did Jesus just call this woman a dog?

It sounds harsh, but there's more going on here. Jesus wasn't insulting her; He was pointing out the divide between Jews and Gentiles. His mission was first to the Jewish people and then to the Gentiles, but this woman's faith was so strong that she refused to give up. She wasn't concerned with cultural barriers—she believed in Jesus and trusted Him to help her, no matter what.

Instead of being offended, the woman responds with humility and belief. She continues to trust, saying, "That's true, Lord, but even the dogs under the table are allowed to eat the scraps from the children's plates." She knew that even a tiny bit of Jesus' power was enough to heal her daughter. And Jesus was moved by her faith. The gospel of Matthew recounts this same story and Jesus replies, "Woman, you have great faith! Your request is granted."[19] Instantly, her daughter was healed. All it took was faith.

Heart check: Today, you and I have a choice to make. We can choose to let our background, past, or any number of excuses keep us from fully trusting God and remain in unbelief—or we can run to Him with childlike trust. Hebrews 4:16 says, "So let us come boldly to the throne of our gracious God. There we will receive his mercy, and we will find grace to help us when we need it most."

PRAYER

God, I want to trust You in all things. Help me live a life fully trusting You instead of living a life in unbelief.

BRING IT HOME

What would happen if I fully trusted Jesus? What would I ask Him to transform in my life?

let's talk about what comes out of your heart

DAY 5

"FOR OUT OF THE ABUNDANCE OF THE HEART HIS **MOUTH SPEAKS**."

—LUKE 6:45, NKJV

Imagine your heart as a giant treasure chest filled with sparkly-gold-glistening multicolored gems. The contents are beautiful, but the best part about this treasure chest is that it is endless! You'll never run out of wealth to put inside it **if** you choose to do so. That means you can continuously give away treasure without running out!

When we put the word of God in our hearts, it's like storing up treasure that we can access at any time. It's a treasure that keeps on giving—a well that will never run dry, blessing our lives and the lives of those around us.

For the last day of this week, let's do a heart check on our **words**. If you want a picture of what's in your heart, start by paying attention to your words. What you say is a great indication of what's in your heart. Are you constantly gossiping about your friend? Complaining about that family member who annoys you? Are you perpetually negative about that situation at school or work? Or are you daily down on yourself, with negative self-talk playing on repeat? Sometimes, we don't know we have a certain belief or attitude until we say something and then the proof is right there, staring us in the face.

Your words have a lot more power than you might give them credit for. God spoke a word and created the universe. With a word, He created you, too. As a daughter who is made in His image, He gave you the creative power to build up or tear down with your words as well. The Bible tells us that death and life are in the power of the tongue.[20]

When I am constantly negative with my words towards myself, others, and God, it's a good indication that my heart is out of alignment with the fully loved daughter He has created me to be. Let's end by declaring what David did in Psalm 19:14: "May the words of my mouth and the meditation of my heart be pleasing to you, O LORD."

Heart check: Watch your words. When you guard the treasury of your heart and deposit good things like the Word of God into it, unending good life will overflow out of you! Through the words you say, you can speak life to the things God wants to bring to every person you encounter.

PRAYER

God, I want my words to reflect the love You have for me and the love You have for others. Thank you for showing me that my words are an indicator of the condition of my heart. Help me live in the reality that I am fully loved by You.

BRING IT HOME

What words have been overflowing from the treasury of my heart recently? What people and situations can I speak life into this week?

Heart check

What words have been overflowing from my heart lately?

- ☐ gossip
- ☐ encouragement
- ☐ complaining
- ☐ kindness
- ☐ negativity
- ☐ words of life

What people and situations can I speak life into this week?

Closing remarks

We hope you have enjoyed this Living Loved journey with God and other friends in the faith. By now, you should know how much God loves you and that your heart is valuable and precious in His eyes. We trust the scripture has come alive to you these past eight weeks and that they have taught you how to guard your heart. Your journey with God is only going to get better with time.

In the weeks to come, remember: your relationship with God is like any other relationship in life. In order to grow the relationship, you need to spend time together. Give God the best of who you are—He won't disappoint. Dive into His Word and discover a million promises that are yours for the taking. Your purpose in God is too great for you to live with anything less than all-in devotion to God. Let Him teach you how to live fully loved in Him.

And know today, sweet daughter, that you are loved and known by God. You are beautiful and perfectly chosen. This is your reality.

There are people on this end of the story who are praying for you and see with God-given perspective the beautiful creation that you are and will become. We are championing God's best in you. We love you. We are here for you. We are cheering you on in your faith-walk with God. Praying that your identity becomes so secure in Him and His Word, you will stand strong, courageous, and grounded in Christ—no matter what comes your way.

Live Loved, precious friend.

Jamie

PS: Feel free to reach out anytime at hello@jamieklusacek.com

Salvation Prayer

I couldn't end this book without giving you the opportunity to pray and commit your life to Jesus. My prayer is that you have seen His love for you woven intricately throughout these pages and felt His desire for you specifically in every chapter.

Having a relationship with Jesus is the best decision you could ever make. The Bible says in Romans 10:9-10 that if we confess with our mouth that Jesus is Lord and believe in our heart God raised Him from the dead, we will be saved.

Join me in the following prayer, asking Jesus to be Lord of our lives:
Jesus, I admit my need for You. I believe that You are God, that You died on the cross for my sins and rose again. I invite You to be Lord of my life. I surrender to You my hopes, my dreams, my hurts, and my wounds. All that I am, I lay at Your feet. Take control of my life and make something beautiful. In Jesus' name, amen.

Whether you have prayed that prayer for the first time or the tenth time, I am celebrating with you today. Start reading your Bible and praying daily. Get to know God, and approach Him like you would any other friendship in your life. Spend time with Him. Find a great church and surround yourself with other people that can bring out God's best in you.

The journey has just begun...

ABOUT THE AUTHORS

Jamie Klusacek

Jamie Klusacek is an author and speaker who lives in Colorado with her amazing Czech-born husband, Milan, and four gorgeous daughters, Grace, Anna, Selah, and Noella. Her primary passion is to love God and love people—to walk courageously obedient with Jesus and help others do the same. She believes that God is near and still speaks personally to us today. Each of our lives is marked for miracles as we join in this adventure to make His name known throughout the earth. Whether serving at her local church, drinking steaming hot tea and writing books, singing bedtime lullabies to her daughters, or baking chocolate chip cookies with friends—Jamie believes that each day is a gift to be cherished, holding opportunities for us to share the genuineness of God's love with those around us. She would love to hear from you.

CONNECT WITH JAMIE

Website
jamieklusacek.com

Email or speaking inquiries
hello@jamieklusacek.com

Instagram
@jamieklusacek

Podcast
Divine Table Talk

ABOUT THE AUTHORS

Hannah Grieser

Ever since Hannah could hold a pencil, she has loved writing and hearing people's stories. Currently, she runs Milk & Honey Content Creation, a company focused on magnifying the message of others through ghostwriting and editing services. Hannah is passionate about spreading truth through the written word and has ghostwritten four books and several devotionals. In her free time, Hannah enjoys spending time with her husband Mason, son John Esli, and dog Gabe, cooking, and doing pretty much anything in the sunshine.

CONNECT WITH HANNAH

Website
milkandhoneyco.org

Writing inquiries
milkandhoneycontent@gmail.com

Instagram
@hannahegrieser

Acknowledgments

I would love to say thank you first and foremost to God. Without Him, none of this would be possible. Thank You for helping me learn to live fully loved by You.

To Milan, who continually amazes me in his encouragement, support, and creative talent. The book is breathtaking. And to our girls—Grace, Anna, Selah, and Noella—for providing the perfect atmosphere for me to learn how to love teen girls well. You all are a priceless treasure.

To Hannah Grieser, co-author, who jumped on board again with her writing gifts. Grateful for you. God's best is ahead for you and your beautiful family.

Tiffany, Autumn, and the THERE{4} Gathering team, who championed the book from dream to reality for the 2nd year in a row. I'm still blown away by your heart and seeing this next generation impacted by the love of God. It's an honor to serve alongside you.

For Bonnie and Suzanne, our beloved Theologian and Editor. It takes a team and I'm beyond grateful to be surrounded by the best. You are a gift from God.

To all the teen girls out there who allowed us to walk this Living Loved journey together. It's an honor to be a part of your story and walk hand in hand with you on the paths of God's love. You are truly loved by God. Let's walk fully loved together.

Photography

All photos provided by pexels.com unless otherwise noted. Photographers, you continue to inspire me.

Week One
Flower: Pixabay

Week Two
Girl with phone: Cottonbro
Girl on the road: Daniel Duarte

Week Three
Girl on a path: Taryn Elliott
Girl: Lilartsy
Petal background: Karolina Grabowska

Week Four
Love sign: iamloe
Car: Leifbergerson

Week Five
Red hair girl: Bertellifotografia
Flower: Sharefaith

Week Six
Paddleboarding: Jess Vide
Grateful girl: rb-audiovisual

Week Seven
Pink shirt girl: Polina Tankilevitch
Brownie: Brunocurly

Week Eight
Girls: Anastasia Shuraeva

Ending Pages
Closing remarks: Annetnavi
Salvation prayer: Jess Vide
Acknowledgments: Jess Bailey Design
Photography: Jess Vide

Footnotes

[1] What language Did Jesus Speak, centerforisrael.com
[2] Koine Greek, ancientlanguage.com
[3] www.jewfaq.org
[4] 1 John 4:19
[5] Isaiah 55:8-9
[6] Footwashing, crossway.org
[7] Martialartswords.com
[8] Numbers 13:27-28 & 14:4, NLT
[9] Ephesians 3:20
[10] Christianity.com
[11] Peace, Eirene, www.preceptaustin.org
[12] Psalm 37:4, paraphrase
[13] The Power of Thoughts, www.impactcounseling.com
[14] Break Free From 3 Self-Sabotaging ANTs, www.health.harvard.edu
[15] Treasure, Merriam-Webster Dictionary
[16] Amy Bernstein, U.S. News & World Report, July 27, 1992, p. 11
[17] Delight, Merriam-Webster Dictionary
[18] Matthew 23:23, NIV
[19] Matthew 15:28
[20] Proverbs 18:21

All Hebrew and Greek word definitions and references are from two sources: The Hebrew Greek Key Word Study Bible (AMG Publishers), and blueletterbible.org.

All scripture references are from the New Living Translation Bible, unless otherwise noted.

We hope you use these resources to continue your personal studies of God's Word.

Other Resources

Choose Truth

This 6-week devotional is written to combat six of the most common lies teen girls face with the Truth of God's Word. As you journey through the pages, may you be reminded of the promises of God for YOUR life. May you exchange your faulty truth for His life-giving Truth. And as you release the lies you believe about yourself, may you find a fresh, heavenly perspective that only YOUR Father in heaven can give.

Remember: You are loved just as you are. You are worthy just as you are. Your life has a great purpose. You are cherished. You are beautiful. God loves you and He's surrounding you with people who love you **too**.

Available on Amazon or jamieklusacek.com

you are **LOVED**